LIGHT

AND

LIVELY

A READER

A READER

LIGHT

AND

LIVELY

MIRA B. FELDER
Borough of Manhattan Community College of the City University of New York

ANNA BRYKS BROMBERG
Brooklyn College of the City University of New York

HARCOURT BRACE JOVANOVICH, INC.

New York   San Diego   Chicago   San Francisco   Atlanta

ISBN: 0-15-550900-4

Library of Congress Catalog Card Number: 79-87868

Printed in the United States of America

Chapter opening illustrations

1	Al Lorenz	83	Warren Lieberman
13	Ron DiScenza	93	Jerry McDaniel
25	Charles Fellows	107	Terry K. Schwarz
39	Jon McIntosh	117	Cindy Ferrara
53	Don Freeman	127	Stuart Leeds
63	David Lindroth	137	Hal Just
75	Michele Maldeau	147	Terry K. Schwarz

Pictorial glosses by Terry K. Schwarz.
Drawings on page 122 by Cindy Ferrara.

PREFACE

We have tried to make *Light and Lively* live up to its name as well as be useful as a text for intermediate students of English as a second language. The book consists of humorous readings accompanied by easy to moderately difficult exercises and it is also suitable for community college freshmen and for students who do not speak standard English.

Light and Lively contains a wide range of humorous stories, generously glossed, and a variety of exercises in vocabulary, grammar, and sentence structure. Besides being entertaining, the stories introduce students to American literature and life. While reading classics of the modern comic tradition (by such writers as Samuel Clemens, Dorothy Parker, James Thurber, William Saroyan, and Art Buchwald) they learn idiomatic expressions and vocabulary connected with everyday American activities and pastimes. (Two pieces by the Canadian writer Stephen Leacock are included because of their universal appeal.) We have included stories about traveling, banking, shopping, making formal complaints, attending university, being on time, and even wasting time. The stories, moreover, are complete and unadapted, so students can learn to appreciate the particular literary style of each work.

All the selections and exercises in the text have been extensively tested in classrooms. They are the product of many hours of teaching and experimentation both by us and by our instructor-consultants, who suggested a number of topics that would make the book more relevant to their students' needs. The exercises, which grow directly out of the stories, stress the most common communication and grammatical problems students face. Comprehension questions (both factual and inferential), vocabulary and idiom exercises, and writing and discussion topics appear in every chapter.

Light and Lively is organized so that it can be used both as a literary anthology and as a grammar text; for either purpose, each chapter is self-contained and requires no additional materials.

We were fortunate to have had these selections and exercises reviewed by several people who gave generously of their time and expertise, especially Shirley Braun of Rockefeller University and Ann Raimes of Hunter College of the City University of New York; Marcia Cohen and Miriam Dancy, both of New York University, were also most helpful in this respect. We also wish to thank Mary Fjeldstad of Manhattan Community College for her numerous suggestions and practical input. At Harcourt

Brace Jovanovich we would like to thank William A. Pullin, Consultant, for his encouragement and suggestions, and for always being there when we needed him. Our thanks also go to Mary Ann De Joseph and Jo Ann Soto, who typed the manuscript.

No book gets written without a great deal of help from family members. We are grateful to our parents, Harry and Fryda, and Sam and Shirley, who successfully mastered the English language without the aid of our text, Howard Bryks, who efficiently collated the Glossary, and our children, Joseph, Sara, and Aaron Felder and Brian and Benjamin Bromberg, who enthusiastically commented on all aspects of *Light and Lively*. The most put-upon members of our families have been our husbands— Simon Felder, who arranged for the typing of the manuscript and helped in the selection-hunting process, and Sol Bromberg, who gave unstintingly of himself and remained convinced that all would go well.

We add a special note of thanks to Art Buchwald, who has proved himself a special friend of the students for whom this book is intended by donating two of his fine pieces to our text.

MIRA B. FELDER

ANNA BRYKS BROMBERG

CONTENTS

Old Country Advice to the American Traveler   William Saroyan   53

This Year It's Going to Be Different   Will Stanton   63

A Bird in Hand—What's It Worth?   Elaine Hart Messmer   75

You Were Perfectly Fine   Dorothy Parker   83

Harpist on Horseback   Hilda Cole Espy   93

The Awful Fate of Melpomenus Jones   Stephen Leacock   107

INTRODUCTION

Light and Lively is an anthology of humorous stories and essays, most of them no more than three pages in length, that will give students a glimpse of American life and American idioms. Each selection is followed by comprehension questions, vocabulary and idiom exercises, and writing and discussion questions, in addition to a variety of grammatical exercises.

The selections are arranged in order of difficulty, with the easier, shorter pieces at the beginning of the text and the longer, more advanced ones at the end. (The last selection, "University Days," is too long to cover in one lesson and has been divided into two parts, each with its own exercises.) When two selections deal with similar topics and can be profitably used for comparison and contrast, they are placed in sequence. For example, "The Soft Sell," which is fairly easy, directly precedes the more advanced "Glove Purchase in Gibraltar" because they both examine the psychology of salesmanship.

The selections may be read in any order of the instructor's preference, since all the difficult words and expressions in every story are defined, even if they have appeared previously in another selection. Thus each chapter is a self-contained unit. Only the verb exercises are arranged in order of difficulty and build on each other as the text progresses. Therefore, if the selections are not being studied in sequence, we recommend that an instructor skip a story occasionally but not go back and forth in the text. Furthermore, the selections go from fairly simple to more complex sentence structures, so some orderly sequence is necessary. Basically, though, every chapter can be used independently to fit the instructor's preferences or students' needs.

VOCABULARY

All words and phrases not easily understood from their context are defined in each selection, even though they may have appeared and been glossed previously. If there are multiple meanings for any word or expression, we have provided all of them, with the first definition a synonym for the word as it is used in the text, so that the student can usually make a direct substitute of the definition for the word being defined.

We use three methods for defining the vocabulary and idioms: (1) New or difficult words are marked in the text by a bubble (°) and are defined in the margin. (2) Idioms and phrases are indicated by an asterisk (*) and are defined in a list at the end of the story. Students should review that list before beginning to read each selection. (3) Finally, for a few other, more complex words and expressions, we have used small pictorial glosses with labels, which appear on the same or facing page.

The opening illustration for each selection aids in defining the title or in illuminating the sense of the piece. For instance, the sketch for "The Romance of a Busy Broker" shows a ticker tape, a telephone, and a typewriter—all equipment used in a brokerage house.

EXERCISES

The exercises, which are short and varied, are designed for maximum student participation. They not only call for standard fill-in and substitution-type answers, but will familiarize students with various American institutions and everyday situations.

Comprehension Questions   These review the student's understanding of the main idea and details of the story; inferential questions test for attention to nuances. The student must always respond in complete sentences, orally or in writing; a simple yes or no is not sufficient.

Vocabulary   Since word and phrase acquisition have the greatest priority for a language student, varied vocabulary exercises appear after each selection to help reinforce the use of new words and expressions. These include fill-in, substitution, and dictionary exercises—both in and out of sentence context. Idiom exercises give students an opportunity to generate original sentences following the example of a particular idiomatic structure.

Articles, Prepositions, and Word Forms   One problem common to students of the English language is mastering the correct use of articles, prepositions, and word endings. To this end we have included many related exercises throughout the text, and we suggest that students read each completed sentence aloud in order to become accustomed to the correct usage.

Verbs   The verb exercises deal with a wide range of skills, from knowing the simple past tense of regular verbs (something students may have aleady learned) to composing complete structures, such as the conditional and perfect tenses, from a model. The exercises test many different aspects of verb competence, including subject-verb agreement, regular and irregular endings, and the correct use of active and passive voice, imperatives, infinitives, and gerunds.

Sentence Structure   Most selections are followed by at least one structure exercise or pattern drill. These become increasingly difficult as the text progresses, and range from simple sentence combining to parallel structure, subordination, and the use of the subjunctive mood.

Other Exercises   Many of the readings contain instances of particular grammatical or structural points that require elaboration and further study. These points are dealt with in exercises that treat tag endings, proverbs, direct and indirect objects, adjectives and adverbs, nationalities and languages, courses of study, the use of "will" and "would," punctuation, spelling, direct and indirect quotations, and forms of obligation.

Topics for Writing and Discussion   Every group of exercises contains suggestions for writing and discussion. Although generated by the selections, they can also be used for more general assignments drawing on students' own experiences. In many cases, an answer will require the use of a specific rhetorical device, such as simple listing, comparison–contrast, and the like, and can take the form of an oral presentation or written assignment.

Special Activities   These exercises engage students in practical, real-life situations suggested by the readings, including shopping, writing letters, filling out bank forms and checks, and role-playing. They call for the application of language skills developed in other lessons throughout the text.

GLOSSARY AND ANSWER KEY

For quick review and easy reference, a Glossary and an Answer Key are printed at the end of the book. The Glossary is an alphabetical listing of all the words and idioms defined in the text, together with a reference to the pages on which they appear. Parts of speech and short definitions have been included as needed for clarity.

The Answer Key enables the instructor to assign independent work (such as a specific grammatical exercise for review or reinforcement), knowing that the student can check his or her own answers and make corrections where necessary.

Complaint Department*

KATHERINE BEST

Katherine Best is a magazine writer whose stories have appeared in many American publications and collections of humor. She writes about the humorous difficulties encountered in everyday experiences. The following selection, taken from a collection called *The Family Book of Humor* (1958), illustrates one difficulty in dealing with a large department store.

M R. SEELEY SHUT HIMSELF IN* the telephone booth. He had a small matter of business to transact° with T. J. Tinglefooter & Co.

    conduct

"Raymond 9-4000," he said to the operator.

"Good afternoon," a smooth voice greeted him. "T. J. Tinglefooter & Co."

"About three days ago," said Mr. Seeley, "my wife bought some flour at your store. . . ."

"Just a moment, sir," the smooth voice said, "I'll connect you with the grocery department."

"Good afternoon. Grocery department, T. J. Tinglefooter & Co.," said another smooth voice.

"Yes," said Mr. Seeley. "I want to tell you about some flour my wife bought. . . ."

"What is the name, please?"

"Mrs. F. D. Seeley. S-E-E-L-E-Y. 479 Crosswood Avenue, Bronxville, New York. This flour you sent, it had worms°."

    worms

"Do you wish to register° a complaint?"

    report

"I certainly do," said Mr. Seeley. "It had worms!"

"Just a moment, sir. I'll connect you with the complaint department."

"Good afternoon," said the complaint department, "T. J. Tinglefooter & Co."

"Is this the worm department?" asked Mr. Seeley.

"I beg your pardon*."

"I ordered some flour from you people and it was all molded or something. It had worms and I want . . ."

"Will you spell it, please?"

"Worms. W-O-R-M-S," spelled Mr. Seeley.

"And what is the nature° of the complaint, Mr. Worms?"

    type

"Worms! *That's* not *my* name! *My* name is Seeley. S-E-E-L-E-Y. 479 Crosswood Avenue, Bronxville, New York."

"And the initials?"

"F. as in Frank, D. as in David."

"Thank you. What is the street address, please?"

"I just *gave* it to you. 479 Crosswood Avenue, Bronxville, New York. You know, four as in one, two, three, four. Seven as in one, two, three, four, five, six. . . ."

"Four, seven, nyun Crosswood Avenue. Thank you. And the town, please?"

"Bronxville. *Bronxville.* And unless those worms have carried it away, it's in New York State."

"Just a moment, Mr. Seeley. You did not receive the merchandise you purchased?"

"I *did!*" shouted Mr. Seeley. "The stuff was crawly° with worms. It was spoiled, see? *Spoiled.* It had worms!" — full; crawling

"Do you wish a readjustment°?" — correction; replacement

"I most certainly do!" Mr. Seeley wiped the perspiration° from his face. "I didn't order worms. I ordered flour." — sweat

"Just a moment, sir. I'll connect you with the readjustment department."

"Good afternoon. Readjustment department, T. J. Tinglefooter & Co." The voices were getting smoother.

"I have worms," said Mr. Seeley desolately°. — hopelessly

"I beg your pardon, sir. What department did you wish."

"I don't know. It's like this*. My wife ordered some flour and it had worms crawling all through it and I called up* to see if you . . ."

"May I have your name, please?"

"F. D. Partment."

"Your street address?"

"794 Bronxwood Avenue."

"Your town?"

"Crossville."

"Your state°?" — a territorial unit of the United States; the way a person feels, someone's condition / very / language disrespectful of God

"Damned° bad." Mr Seeley rarely resorted to* blasphemy°.

"I beg your pardon. What number did you call?"

"New York."

"Thank you. What is the nature of the complaint?"

"You see, my wife bought the loveliest sack of flour you ever saw. It was all wrapped up in pretty white paper and we could hardly wait to open it. And what do you suppose had gotten in our lovely white sack of flour? Worms, old nasty°, crawly worms." Mr. Seeley writhed° in reminiscence°. — dirty; unpleasant / twisted / remembrance

"The merchandise was received in imperfect condition? Very good. What readjustment do you wish?"

"I want you to send me," said Mr. Seeley wearily, "some more flour without imperfect conditions crawling all around in it."

"Just a moment, sir. I'll connect you with the order depart . . ."

Mr. Seeley left the telephone booth and went fishing.

IDIOMS AND PHRASES*

complaint department	*an office set up by most large stores to deal with dissatisfied customers*
shut himself in	*went in and closed the door*
I beg your pardon	*please repeat; excuse me*
it's like this	*this is the situation*
called up	*telephoned*
resorted to	*turned to*

A

COMPREHENSION QUESTIONS

1. What was the problem that Mr. Seeley was complaining about?

2. What was the information that all of the people asked of Mr. Seeley? Why?

3. Why did Mr. Seeley have so much trouble explaining his problem?

4. Name the ways in which T. J. Tinglefooter & Co. can satisfy Mr. Seeley's complaint. What does Mr. Seeley want?

5. Did the person in the readjustment department use the word "state" in the way that Mr. Seeley understood it? How do you know?

6. Would Mr. Seeley have been more successful in replacing his wormy flour if he had written a letter of complaint? Why?

7. Why did Mr. Seeley give up?

8. What made Mr. Seeley think of going fishing?

B

VOCABULARY BUILDER

Fill in each blank with a word from the list below.

reminiscence	crawly	damned
transacts	readjustment	resorted to

nasty   perspiration   blasphemy
worms   desolately   writhed
nature   state

Example: Although Mr. Seeley thinks that worms are _____
crawling creatures, he uses them to catch fish.

Although Mr. Seeley thinks that worms are <u>nasty</u> crawling creatures, he uses them to catch fish.

1. She _____ all of her business over the telephone.

2. What is the _____ of your problem?

3. When she found a mistake in her bill, the woman asked for a _____.

4. The _____ on his forehead was caused by running to catch the bus.

5. The student received his failing grade _____.

6. What is the _____ of your health?

7. She was so angry that she _____ shouting.

8. We are taught in school that _____ is wrong.

9. After the accident, the victim _____ in pain while waiting for the ambulance.

10. My _____ of home is very pleasant.

11. Mr. Seeley complained because the flour was _____ with

_____.

Idioms: I beg your pardon
It's like this

12. " _____," he said. "Can you tell me how to get to the subway?"

13. "_____," the customer said. "You sent me the wrong size shirt."

C

SENTENCE BUILDER

Use each phrase in an original sentence.

Example: connect with

> **Mr. Seeley said to the operator, "Please <u>connect</u> me <u>with</u> the complaint department."**

1. I beg your pardon
2. it's like this
3. register a complaint
4. I want to tell you about
5. I called up
6. resorted to
7. we could hardly wait to
8. what do you suppose

D

WORD FORMS

Fill in the correct form of the words listed below.

1. connect, connecting, connection

   a. Can you find a _____ between worms and fishing?

   b. For better radio reception, _____ these wires to the outdoor antenna.

   c. We missed our _____ flight and had to wait for three more hours.

2. transact, transacting, transaction

   a. I have important business to _____ with you.

   b. He didn't know that a simple complaint would turn into such a difficult

   _____ .

   c. We will not be _____ any business on Lincoln's Birthday.

3. wrap, wrapper, wrapping

   a. Joseph chose _____ paper to

           _____ the gifts he had bought.

   b. _____ your packages carefully before mailing them.

   c. The person who _____ packages in a department store

      is called a _____ .

   d. The _____ on the chewing gum keeps it fresh.

   e. While he was _____ the alarm clock, it started to ring.

E

TAG ENDINGS

Fill in the appropriate tag endings, making sure that pronoun and verb agree.

Example: They're very nice, _____?

    They're very nice, <u>aren't they?</u>

1. He's tall, _____?

2. She's beautiful, _____?

3. We were leaving, _____?

4. They're Russians, _____?

5. I was invited, _____?

6. You will come, _____?

7. You can do it, _____?

8. You're pleased with your gift, _____?

9. You were home, _____?

10. We will have enough food, _____?

F

"SAY" AND "TELL"

Supply the correct form of **say** or **tell** in the following sentences.

1. Mary _____ that she was too tired to go to the library with me.

2. Mary _____ me that she was too tired to go to the library with me.

3. I _____ my teacher that I could not finish my work in time.

4. Jane _____ me all about her class. She _____ that it was very interesting.

5. Patricia _____ that the scarf belonged to her sister.

6. I _____ her that I thought it belonged to Helen.

7. Will you please _____ me what time it is?

8. Please don't _____ me you can't come to my party.

9. What else can I _____?

10. What did he _____ about the job?

11. The coach always _____ the team to try harder.

12. Shall I _____ you what I think of this idea?

13. When he calls, will you please _____ that I am out?

14. When he calls, please _____ him that I will be back in an hour.

15. Grace _____ to me, "I shall never marry him."

G

VERB TENSES

Fill in the blank with the correct form of the verb below the line.

1. Please _____ away.
(go)

2. He _____ to the store yesterday.
(go)

3. Tomorrow when she _____ to the store, she
(go)

_____ flour.
(buy)

4. Yesterday he _____ his girlfriend a watch.
(buy)

5. It usually _____ two people to carry the sofa.
(take)

6. He _____ a nap when she called him.
(take)

7. _____ slowly when you pass a playground.
(drive)

8. While _____ in the country, I ran out of gas.
(drive)

9. Last week we _____ to the beach.
(drive)

10. The actress _____ the stage angrily.
(leave)

11. Let's _____ early to avoid the traffic.
(leave)

12. As he _____ the house, he heard the telephone
(leave)
ring.

13. Now I _____ of you very often.
(think)

14. I _____ the play was very good but the acting was
(think)
amateurish.

15. Were you _____ of me when you wrote the poem?
(think)

16. Why did you _____ him the keys to the car?
(give)

17. Last night he _____ the car back to me.
(give)

18. Tomorrow the professor _____ a lecture on American
(give)
history.

19. _____ if you can find this address for me.
(see)

20. Last week we _____ an interesting exhibit in the
(see)
museum.

21. I _____ John at the party tomorrow evening.
(see)

H

DIRECT AND INDIRECT SPEECH

Change each sentence from direct to indirect speech.

Example: The nurse said to us, "Don't come back until one o'clock."

The nurse told us not to come back until one o'clock.

1. "Please give me more candy," Jamie said to his mother.

2. "No, it's not good for you," Mother said.

3. Mr. Seeley said to the operator, "I wish to register a complaint."

4. She replied, "I will connect you with the complaint department."

5. "There are worms in my flour," said Mr. Seeley.

6. Lois said to me, "I always let people get ahead of me on checkout lines in the supermarket."

7. The tour guide advised the tourists, "If you get to the bus early, you will be sure to get a seat."

8. "Don't approach the gorilla," the zoo keeper warned. "He may grab your tie."

9. "Running is a good form of exercise," the doctor said to his patient.

10. "She is very uncooperative," Mr. Seeley complained to the manager.

I

STRUCTURES

Rewrite the sentences below by using the suggested pattern.

1. *Pattern:* I'm sorry I called so late. → **I beg your pardon. I didn't mean to call so late.**

   a. I'm sorry I stepped on your toes.

   b. I regret that I hurt your feelings.

   c. I took your pencil by mistake.

2. *Pattern:* Let's discuss my problems with my landlord. → **I want to tell you about my problems with my landlord.**

    a. Let's talk about my boyfriend.

    b. Let's discuss my meeting with John.

    c. I want to explain my problem with the complaint department.

3. *Pattern:* They were looking forward to spring vacation. → **They could hardly wait for spring vacation.**

    a. They were anxious to see Jane.

    b. We were eagerly expecting the delivery of our new rings.

    c. I am eager to see how the new coat I bought for Tommy fits him.

J

TOPICS FOR WRITING AND DISCUSSION

1. Describe a problem or misunderstanding you have had with a store. How did you handle it?

2. Most bills are now prepared by computers. Have you ever had a problem with a computer-prepared bill?

3. Write a letter of complaint about a problem that you have had with a store, or write a letter explaining Mr. Seeley's problem.

4. Prepare a five-minute presentation on how to get a refund on your merchandise from a department store.

5. Pretend you are the manager of a complaint department. How would you deal with Mr. Seeley's wormy flour? Try acting out the scene with a classmate.

The Time Killer

ART BUCHWALD

Art Buchwald (1925–), a native New Yorker, first became known when he was a Paris-based columnist for the *New York Herald-Tribune*. After leaving Paris, he settled in Washington, D.C., and started writing satirically humorous articles about American politics. His syndicated column appears in over four hundred newspapers, and he is noted for his commentaries on politics and contemporary customs. Among his books are *I Never Danced at the White House* (1973) and *I Am Not a Crook* (1974). The selection below, from *More Caviar* (1957), focuses on the great interest Americans have in European travel.

ACCORDING TO* NUNNALLY JOHNSON, the Hollywood director and writer, the hardest thing for a male tourist in Europe to do is kill time*.

"There is absolutely nothing for a guy to do in Paris," said Mr. Johnson, "if he is not interested in sightseeing or going shopping with his wife."

Mr. Johnson claims° to be an expert on killing time in Paris and thought he might be able to advise other husbands who are bent on* doing the same thing.

says, states

"The first thing to do," said Mr. Johnson, "is to clear your day. Don't make any appointments that might interfere with* your time killing.

"It will take about one hour to get your wife off on her shopping excursion. You can kill some time with her explaining the franc equivalents° of dollars and discussing where you'll meet her for lunch. It isn't the best way of killing time, but it has to be done. Once she is out of the way you can become serious.

the same values

"One of the best ways I've found of killing time in Paris is to look for someone you know is in the city, but you're not sure where he is staying. I go from hotel to hotel asking for him. Usually I look for someone I'm not very interested in finding, so if I happen to find where he is staying, then I can start looking for someone else.

"Some days when I can't think of anyone to look for, I look at the list of arrivals at the American Express which are printed in the *Herald Tribune*. The other day I saw: 'I. Rappaport of Detroit.' I once knew an Irving Rappaport in Atlanta, Georgia, but he could have very well moved to Detroit. Although I spoke to him only once at my brother's wedding, I distinctly° remember him saying he didn't like Atlanta and was thinking of moving.

clearly, definitely

"So I called the American Express, which took an hour in

itself, and asked them if the I. Rappaport of Detroit reported in the papers could possibly be Irving Rappaport who used to live in Atlanta. The girl said she didn't know, so I said I would come down and look at the book myself. She said this was all right with her.

"Well, it took me an hour by taxi to get there, and then it took me a half hour deciding whether to buy *Time* Magazine or *Newsweek*, which were on sale in front of the building. Then I went in and asked to see the register°. I started looking through it slowly, reading a lot of other names, and finally, after a half an hour, I came to Rappaport's name. But it was Ida Rappaport, and I distinctly remember Irving's wife was named Sarah. All told* it killed three hours, which I was very grateful for.

°record book

"Another way of killing time is to go to different places and check to see if there is any mail for you. You can go to American Express, Thomas Cook, Morgan's bank, TWA and the American Embassy, all mail drops* for American tourists. If you make the rounds* on foot it can kill two and a half hours easily.

"If you have a couple of hours to go, you can always stop in to a plane or ship reservation office and inquire° about a trip you have no intention of taking. To do it properly you must inquire about schedules° and make the reservation clerk constantly check his timetable°. If you haven't killed enough time you might ask about making a connection* with another airline or a train.

°ask

schedules, timetable; listings of arrival and departure times

"One of the most successful methods of killing time is to pay your respects* to the Paris branch office of your company. You call up the manager and tell him you're in town for a few days and would like to stop by and say hello. In any case* I go to Twentieth Century-Fox. Sometimes there are other people waiting to pay their respects, but I'm not in a hurry. The fact you have to wait serves a purpose* in itself. Once you're in the manager's office you can ask any questions you want to about the operation°, and since you're from the home office and he doesn't know how you stand with* his boss, the manager has to answer them. I once killed two and a half hours by simply asking the Twentieth Century-Fox man: 'How do you dub° pictures into French?'

°business

°add the voices or sounds to a film

"Another time I killed four hours by asking: 'Why does France keep changing its premiers?' "

When Mr. Johnson has run out of ideas he sits in his room and sulks° about his wife's shopping. This can kill some time, but it isn't healthy time killing, because if he thinks about it too long he gets mad°.

°shows displeasure silently

°angry

I spent about two hours with him and he was very grateful° to me. He said as soon as I left he was going to call up a French

°thankful

producer° and discuss a co-production with him. "I have no inten-   film maker
tion of making it," he said, "but I know if we start discussing
money I'll get through the afternoon. If not, I think I'll look up Ida
Rappaport. It's very possible she could be Irving's sister."

IDIOMS AND PHRASES*

according to	*on the word or authority of*
kill time	*pass time idly or unproductively*
bent on	*determined*
interfere with	*get in the way of*
all told	*including everything*
mail drops	*addresses where a tourist can receive mail*
make the rounds	*follow a usual route*
making a connection	*transferring to another plane or train*
pay your respects	*make a courtesy call*
in any case	*no matter what happens, anyhow*
serves a purpose	*meets a need or requirement*
how you stand with	*the position you have in the organization (or in the relationship)*

A

COMPREHENSION QUESTIONS

1. What two activities do not interest Mr. Johnson?

2. What advice does Mr. Johnson give his wife before she leaves for her shopping trip?

3. Who is I. Rappaport?

4. What was Irving's wife's first name?

5. What offices handle tourist mail?

6. To whom does Mr. Johnson pay his respects?

7. Does Mr. Johnson want to produce a movie?

8. Do you think Mr. Johnson likes being a tourist? Why?

B

VOCABULARY BUILDER

Match each word in the first column with the word or phrase in the second column that is closest to it in meaning.

1. interfere with (v.)	**a.** question
2. schedule (n.)	**b.** plainly
3. distinctly (adv.)	**c.** timetable
4. operation (n.)	**d.** the same values
5. inquire (v.)	**e.** business
6. grateful (adj.)	**f.** show displeasure silently
7. equivalents (n.)	**g.** thankful
8. mad (adj.)	**h.** get in the way of
9. register (n.)	**i.** guest book
10. sulk (v.)	**j.** angry

C

IDIOMS

Use each of the underlined idioms in another sentence, following the suggested example.

Example: He was <u>bent on</u> finding a job.

    I was bent on finishing the exercise.

1. <u>According to</u> the newspapers, there is a great deal of crime in New York City.

    According to _____.

2. It may snow tomorrow, but we shall drive to Chicago <u>in any case</u>.

    _____ in any case.

3. Once she is <u>out of the way</u>, you can become serious.

    _____ out of the way, _____.

4. <u>All told</u>, we have twenty people on the tour.

All told, _____.

5. You can <u>kill</u> some <u>time</u> by discussing where you'll meet for lunch.

_____ kill time _____.

6. I'm not <u>in a hurry</u> to get married.

_____ in a hurry _____.

7. Do these exercises <u>serve a purpose?</u>

_____ serve a purpose?

D

STATEMENTS AND QUESTIONS

Change each of the following statements to a question.

Example: There is nothing for a man to do in Paris.

    Is there anything for a man to do in Paris?

1. It will take about an hour to explain this to you.

2. It has to be done.

3. You can go to American Express for your mail.

4. I looked at the list of arrivals.

5. Even if he doesn't know you, he has to speak to you.

E

VERB TENSES

Change the underlined verbs in the following sentences from the present tense to the past tense.

Example: He <u>sits</u> in his chair.

    He sat in his chair.

1. He <u>kills</u> time.

_____

2. They <u>go</u> to the movies every week.

_____

3. You <u>find</u> seashells at the seashore.

_____

4. The children <u>speak</u> English well.

_____

5. Mother <u>interferes</u> in my affairs too much.

_____

6. We <u>think</u> he <u>will</u> be all right.

_____

7. The child <u>stops</u> crying when his mother <u>picks</u> him up.

_____

8. The newspaper <u>prints</u> the names of all arrivals.

_____

9. It <u>takes</u> me an hour to get to work.

_____

10. Where <u>do</u> you live?

_____

F

WORD FORMS

Fill in the correct form of the words listed below.

1. report, reporter, reporting

   a. He was only _____ the news.

   b. The _____ wrote a very interesting newspaper article.

   c. Make your _____ short and clear.

2. interfere, interference, interfering

   a. The editors of the school newspaper resented any _____.

   b. Employers should not _____ too much in their workers' private affairs.

   c. The static was _____ with our television reception.

3. discuss, discussion, discussing

   a. They were _____ a new athletic program.

   b. The _____ led to many interesting conclusions.

   c. Please _____ the matter with me before you leave.

4. distinct, distinctly, distinction

   a. I heard him say _____ that he was going to the theater with his girlfriend.

   b. There is a _____ possibility that we shall go to Paris next year.

   c. We make no _____ between an A+ and an A.

5. knowledge, known, knowing, know

   a. Have you _____ him long?

   b. _____ the subject so well, you will easily pass the test.

   c. His _____ of first-aid techniques helped him save the man's life.

   d. Do you _____ the way to the library?

G

REGULAR VERBS

Fill in the correct form of the verb below the line.

1. Mr. Johnson _____ that he knows a famous film producer.

(claim)

2. He _____ American Express yesterday.

(call)

3. Where _____ you _____ then?

(do) (live)

4. Yesterday I _____ overtime.

(work)

5. Mr. Johnson _____ over so that his friend could sit down.

(move)

6. We _____ the name Rappaport wrong yesterday.

(spell)

7. The women _____ very hard when they opened the new school.

(work)

8. I love to listen when she _____ the piano.

(play)

9. He _____ to Detroit last week.

(move)

10. They _____ in New York for two years before they _____ France.

(live)   (visit)

11. In the film I saw yesterday, the tourist _____ the hotel
    (kill)
    manager.

12. Yesterday we _____ where we would meet for lunch.
    (discuss)

13. She _____ in her hotel room for two hours waiting for
    (stay)
    her friend to return.

14. Mr. Johnson _____ when his wife doesn't want to go
    (sulk)
    sightseeing.

H

PREPOSITIONS

Fill in the blanks in the sentences below with the correct preposition from this list: **into,
to, toward, out of, away from.**

1. Mr. Johnson walked _____ the building.

2. She gave the letter _____ him.

3. They ran _____ the hotel when the fire alarm sounded.

4. Mr. Johnson walked _____ the reservations office after inquiring
   about a trip.

5. Mr. Rappaport came _____ me with a big smile on his face.

6. The dog ran _____ me when I sprayed him with water.

7. I saw the mailman walk _____ the American Express office.

8. I enjoy walking _____ work every morning.

9. He opened the door to let me _____ the house.

10. He poured some sugar _____ the sack and _____
    the sugar bowl.

I

ARTICLES

Fill in the blanks below with the article **a, an,** or **the.**

Well, it took me _____ hour by taxi to get there, and then

it took me _____ half-hour to decide whether to buy *Time* or

Newsweek, which were on sale in front of _____ building.

Then I went in and asked to see _____ register. I started

looking through it slowly, reading _____ lot of other names,

and finally, after _____ half _____ hour, I came to Rap-

paport's name.

J

STRUCTURES: -ing VERB FORMS AS ADJECTIVES AND NOUNS

Complete the following sentences by filling in the proper form of the verb below the line.

1. We went here and there _____ how to get to the station.

(ask)

2. They plan to go _____ tomorrow.

(fish)

3. He spends a lot of time _____ for his examinations.

(study)

4. We saw his car _____ down the road.

(come)

5. He heard his mother _____ him for supper.

(call)

6. We listened to the rain _____ on the roof.

(fall)

7. They saw the water _____ down the hill.

(run)

8. He found his sister _____ on the floor.

(lie)

9. They went _____ for ducks last month.
                         (hunt)

10. He lay on his bed _____ of boredom.
                            (die)

11. We have to start _____ up earlier.
                          (get)

12. She is thinking of _____ her hair dyed.
                            (have)

13. He is afraid of _____ before a large audience.
                        (appear)

14. He is an expert on _____ just the right thing to say.
                           (know)

15. They are interested in _____ jobs.
                                (find)

16. Charles is bent on _____ to France next summer.
                           (travel)

17. We have no intention of _____ them win the game.
                                 (let)

18. I am not used to _____ a car.
                         (drive)

19. She was asking about _____ a trip to Spain.
                             (take)

20. I have no intention of _____ up with such behavior.
                               (put)

K

TOPICS FOR WRITING AND DISCUSSION

1. What are some of your personal experiences regarding traveling?

2. What is your concept of the typical American tourist?

3. What is your favorite way of killing time? Can you suggest other time-killing activities for Mr. Johnson?

4. Aside from shopping and sightseeing, what activities could you suggest to Mr. Johnson that would not be time-killing?

The Late Mr. Adams

STEVE ALLEN

Steve Allen (1921–   ), a well-known comedian and television performer, is also the author of more than a dozen books and some three thousand songs. Born in New York City into a vaudeville family, he lived with a number of aunts and attended eighteen schools before his graduation from high school. He writes poetry, novels, and nonfiction and can play almost any musical instrument. Allen has written of his many talents in his autobiography, *Mark It and Strike It* (1960). The following selection is taken from a collection of his stories, *Fourteen for Tonight* (1955).

MR. ADAMS, TO GET RIGHT TO THE POINT, was born late. The doctor had solemnly° wiped his spectacles°, pursed° his lips, made the sort of face all doctors are supposed to make after wiping their spectacles and pursing their lips, and announced that George Adams would be born on August 23. *with dignity, seriously / eyeglasses / pulled tightly together*

On August 22 his mother felt pains and retired° to await George's arrival. On August 29 the doctor suggested light housework and a change of diet, reexamined his calculations, and stated with assured° finality that George would be born within two days. George was born seven days later. *went to bed / certain*

Till the day he died George loved to tell the story of his long-delayed arrival, and I suppose psychologists might suggest that his lifelong addiction° to tardiness° was a subconscious means of recapturing the glory, such as it was, that was his on the occasion of his birth. *bad habit / lateness*

They say that the worst thief in the world is an honest man 99 per cent of the time. They say that except on certain days of the week Hitler wasn't an altogether unlikable sort of chap°. They say that all beautiful women have their unattractive moments, that saints sometimes sin, and that the New York Yankees don't always defeat their opponents from Philadelphia. *man*

They say that nobody runs entirely true to type*. But they are wrong. George Adams was late coming into this world, he was late being weaned°, he was late learning to speak, he was late for school habitually from the first day he attended kindergarten, and with very rare exceptions he was late for every blessed° appointment of any importance that was ever included in his busy schedule. *changed from mother's milk to other food / (slang) damned*

His other vices°, fortunately, were few and of relative unimportance, and his virtues° were many. He always managed somehow to discharge° his educational responsibilities with ease, and when he graduated from the state university he was in the upper tenth of his class. *very bad habits / good qualities / perform*

He was, needless to say*, tardy in arriving at the graduation ceremony, but his dean° was in no way surprised by this circumstance, and George's diploma was handed to him privately after the speechmaking and singing had ended and the janitors° were beginning to fold up the auditorium chairs and put them away.

°dean: administrative officer of a university

°janitors: cleaning men

George's father soon thereafter made an opening at his plant° and George filled it neatly. His father, with great wisdom, instructed George's secretary to lie deliberately° to George regarding the times of all especially important business appointments, so that when George had to meet a business associate° for lunch at one o'clock he usually was given the impression that the engagement was set for twelve-thirty, and so when he sauntered° onto the scene at something like twelve fifty-four there was really no harm done.

°plant: factory

°deliberately: on purpose

°associate: fellow worker

°sauntered: strolled or walked slowly

George made a great many friends as a junior executive° and in no time was promoted and given a substantial° increase in income. While not handsome he was more than slightly attractive, women found him amusing, and so one day when he announced that he was engaged to be married the news was not entirely unexpected.

°executive: business manager, administrator / °substantial: large

His father, fortunately, had the presence of mind* to warn George's bride that her husband-to-be might arrive a few minutes late for the wedding service, so although she was visibly annoyed° by this eventuality° when it came to pass*, she was not driven to tears° and there was really no scene° at all. Besides, George had the best of excuses: he had stopped to have his car washed and to make a long-distance telephone call to a hotel in New York to make absolutely certain the honeymoon suite* had been reserved.

°annoyed: made angry

°eventuality: possibility

°scene: public display of anger

George usually had a good excuse, as a matter of fact*. He wasn't late on purpose; his intentions were the best in the world. It was just that most of the time, what with one thing and another coming up at the last minute, he never quite seemed to get anywhere as early as he wanted to.

In later years George came to be a prominent° citizen of the town, and there was even talk one year of running° him for mayor. He declined this honor, however, and continued to devote himself to private endeavor. After his father died he assumed° the presidency of the plant and rendered the company distinguished service*. His marriage withal° was a happy one and his children, four in number, were a fine-looking group at the funeral not long ago.

°prominent: important

°running: suggesting (for public office)

°assumed: undertook, accepted

°withal: in addition

Everyone said it was one of the nicest funerals in recent years, and though George's family was heartbroken, you could see they were still able to feel a glow of pride as they looked over the crowd that packed into the church to pay its respects and hear the funeral oration.

I suppose there must have been many in the crowd who were aware that, in dying, George Adams was early for almost the first time in his life. His physician, who had detected a serious heart condition, had given him two years to live, at the outside*, and the good doctor was as shocked° as the townspeople when, three weeks after his examination, diagnosis, and prediction, his patient quietly passed away* in his sleep.

unpleasantly surprised

The caravan of sleek°, black limousines winding° to the cemetery was imposing, indeed, and the casual passersby must have concluded that a very important personage was being laid to rest*.

long and shiny / turning

One minor mishap° interrupted the smooth flow of events, incidentally, at what was, to all practical purposes, the very last minute. The hearse° that carried George's coffin must have run over a nail in the road, for one of its tires went suddenly quite flat and the driver and his assistant pulled over to the roadside to replace it with a spare. After a hasty° conference it was decided that all the other cars should proceed, as planned, directly to the burial ground. This they did and the mourners, stepping out of the limousines sedately°, clustered° around the Adams plot and stood conversing in whispers, waiting for George.

accident

funeral car

quick

calmly, seriously / met, gathered in groups

He arrived only 23 minutes late.

IDIOMS AND PHRASES*

runs entirely true to type	*acts as expected*
needless to say	*unnecessary to say*
presence of mind	*awareness, alertness*
came to pass	*happened*
driven to tears	*caused to cry*
honeymoon suite	*deluxe hotel room for newly married people*
as a matter of fact	*really*
rendered the company distinguished service	*benefited or helped it*
at the outside	*and no more*
passed away	*died*
laid to rest	*buried*

A

COMPREHENSION QUESTIONS

1. What advice did the doctor give George's mother?

2. Was George a good student?

3. How did George get his diploma?

4. Why was George late for his wedding?

5. Where did George get a job? What position did he hold?

6. How did George's father make sure George was on time for his appointments?

7. George was early only once in his life. When?

8. How late was George for his funeral? Why?

9. How do you think George could have been taught to be on time?

10. What good qualities did George have to make up for his lateness?

B

VOCABULARY BUILDER

Replace the underlined word in each sentence with the proper synonym from the list below.

important	accident	shiny
bad habit	go to bed	accepted
seriously	very bad habits	intentionally
possibility	late	fellow worker
came together	turning	strolled
calmly	university administrator	good qualities
cleaning man	business administrators	

1. The doctor <u>solemnly</u> wiped his eyeglasses.

2. His other <u>vices</u>, fortunately, were few and of relative unimportance.

3. His father instructed George's secretary to lie <u>deliberately</u> to George regarding the time of all important business appointments.

4. When George had to meet a business <u>associate</u> for lunch at one o'clock, he usually was given the impression that the engagement was set for twelve-thirty.

5. When he <u>sauntered</u> onto the scene at twelve-fifty, there was really no harm done.

6. Although she was visibly annoyed by this <u>eventuality</u> when it came to pass, she was not driven to tears.

7. His <u>virtues</u> were many.

8. In later years George came to be a <u>prominent</u> citizen of the town.

9. The mourners <u>clustered</u> around the Adams plot.

10. After his father died, he <u>assumed</u> the presidency of the plant.

11. Even though she was very proud of her son, she sat <u>sedately</u> at the awards ceremony.

12. Some doctors think smoking is an <u>addiction.</u>

13. The <u>janitor</u> of the apartment house lives on the ground floor.

14. I told the boy who cut his finger that it was only a slight <u>mishap</u>.

15. Please make sure all the doors are locked before you <u>retire</u>.

16. She sent a <u>tardy</u> letter of thanks to her hostess.

17. He drove very slowly and carefully on the <u>winding</u> road.

18. The <u>dean</u> warned him that if his grades did not improve he would be expelled.

19. There was a meeting of all the company <u>executives</u>.

20. He was driving a <u>sleek</u> new sports car.

C

IDIOMS

Use each underlined idiom in another sentence, following the example.

Example: He had enough <u>presence of mind</u> to call the fire department before the fire spread.

<u>She had enough presence of mind to leave the building when the fire started.</u>

1. I don't want to see you today, and, <u>as a matter of fact</u>, I don't want to see you tomorrow either.

_____ and,

as a matter of fact, _____.

2. The teacher's lesson on Proust ran <u>true to type</u> because it was as boring as all his other lessons.

_____ true to type because

_____.

3. He <u>rendered</u> his country a <u>service</u> by fighting in World War II.

_____ rendered a service by

_____.

4. <u>Needless to say</u>, I was very pleased to be going on vacation.

Needless to say, _____

_____.

5. When he drank the medicine, <u>he made a face</u>.

_____ made a face.

D

PRONOUNS

Fill in the blank with the correct pronoun, and give the reason for your choice.

1. The mayor asked _____ to vote for him.
(we/us)

2. They gave _____ two seats up front.
(we/us)

3. This is Mary, _____ will be glad to help you.
(who/whom)

4. _____ do you think will win the election?
(Who/Whom)

5. May _____ help you wash the dishes?
(I/me)

6. Between you and _____, I can't afford a vacation.
(I/me)

7. I have always been able to drive a car better than —————————.
                                                          (she/her)

8. Do you know ——————————— left this note?
                        (who/whom)

9. The old woman left ——————————— all her money.
                              (he/him)

10. Let ——————————— drive to the funeral in two cars.
            (they/them)

E

ACTIVE AND PASSIVE VOICE

Change the sentences below from the passive to the active voice.

Example: George's diploma was handed to him by the dean.

The dean handed George his diploma.

1. He was given the impression by his father that he would be promoted.

2. She was driven to tears by George's lateness.

3. The honeymoon suite had been reserved by George.

4. He was late being weaned by his mother.

5. It was decided by the family that all the other cars should proceed as planned.

6. My car was washed by me last week.

7. This watch is considered by Cathy the best one you can buy.

8. The book was written by a famous French historian.

9. An agreement was reached between labor and management.

10. The baby was bathed and fed by the baby sitter before he was put to bed.

F

ARTICLES

Fill in the article **a, an,** or **the** if it is required.

Examples: She broke ————— vase.   She likes ————— good wine.

She broke _a_ vase.   **She likes good wine.**

_____little boy ran into _____ street.

The little boy ran into the street.

1. He does not have _____ single Beatles record.

2. _____ genius is 10 percent inspiration and 90 percent perspiration.

3. She likes to wear _____ nice clothing.

4. I am studying _____ philosophy of Spinoza.

5. He made _____ delicious omelet.

6. "_____ only thing we have to fear is _____ fear itself."

7. Rockefeller earned _____ great wealth from his oil wells.

8. _____ soccer is _____ sport that is becoming more popular in the United States.

9. Rockefeller amassed _____ great fortune from his oil wells.

10. Because of _____ energy crisis, we must encourage _____ public transportation.

11. He would like to meet _____ beautiful woman.

12. We are _____ nation of immigrants.

13. _____ doctor gave his patient _____ good advice.

14. What _____ good weather we're having today!

15. He is studying _____ philosophy.

G

PREPOSITIONS

Fill in the blanks with the appropriate prepositions from the following list: **at, in, on, to, from, next to, until, after.**

I was born _____ Hungary. _____ my fif-

1
2

teenth birthday, we came _____ New York City. Before

3

we bought our house, we lived _____ 2015 Washington

4

Avenue. It was a small apartment _____ a large build-

5

ing. The neighbors who lived _____ us had three small

6

children, who woke up every Sunday morning _____

7

six o'clock. _____ they had put _____ their

8
9

slippers, they came _____ our door to ask for cookies.

10

They stayed _____ our apartment _____ six

11
12

o'clock _____ ten, when their parents woke up and

13

called them home for breakfast. I have always wondered about

this American custom of sending your children to the neighbors'

when you want to sleep late.

H

PAST PERFECT TENSE

The past perfect tense expresses a past time that comes before another past time.

The students <u>had</u> already <u>left</u> by the time the teacher arrived.
He said that he <u>had left</u> his sweater at home.

Use one past perfect verb and one past verb in each of the following sentences.

Example: Before his father _____ anything to him, the child
                                          (say)
_____ to cry.
            (begin)

   Before his father <u>said</u> anything to him, the child <u>had begun</u> to cry.

  1. After a while he _____ that he _____
                              (realize)   (take)
     the wrong coat.

  2. The secretary _____ the office after she _____
                              (leave)   (type)
     the letters.

  3. They _____ married for five years before they
                    (be)

     _____ a baby.
                  (have)

  4. She _____ to know what he _____.
                    (want)   (buy)

  5. He _____ on a ship until he _____
                  (never be)   (sail)
     to Bermuda.

  6. They _____ the packages that they _____
                    (never receive)   (order)
     from the store.

  7. They always _____ the vacation they _____.
                          (remember)   (take)

  8. They _____ a room before they _____.
                    (reserve)   (arrive)

  9. They _____ the program even after the state
                    (continue)

     _____ their budget.
                  (reduce)

 10. She _____ the piano every day even though she
                    (play)

     _____ taking lessons.
                  (stop)

 11. This past winter _____ much colder than we
                                  (be)

     _____ it to be.
                  (expect)

12. By the time we _____ to the theater, the play already
                           (get)

_____.
          (start)

13. The people who _____ to buy their house
                            (promise)

_____ their minds.
          (change)

14. I _____ that they _____ a
            (not know)   (rent)

summer cottage.

15. I _____ many things about this country before I
            (hear)

_____ here.
          (come)

I

COMPARATIVE ENDINGS

Fill in the correct comparative or superlative form of the adjective in parentheses.

1. He was the _____ student in the class. (good)

2. He was _____ than I at playing chess. (good)

3. She is the _____ in the family. (young)

4. That was the _____ painting I had ever
seen. (beautiful)

5. Her handwriting is _____ than mine. (bad)

6. Spelling is my _____ subject. (bad)

7. She is the _____ person I've ever met. (difficult)

8. There were _____ people at my party than I had
invited. (many)

9. He tried to get by with doing the _____ work. (little)

10. He gave _____ than he could afford. (little)

11. Because she was on a diet, she took the ———————————————— piece of cake. (small)

12. Are you ———————————————— in your new school than in your old one? (happy)

13. That's the ———————————————— dog I ever had. (lazy)

14. She is ———————————————— than I am. (young)

15. As we approached, the noise seemed ————————————————. (loud)

J

TOPICS FOR WRITING AND DISCUSSION

1. Do you know someone who is always late? What excuses does he or she give?

2. Is there a deep psychological reason for constant lateness, or is it just a bad habit?

3. Are you generally late or early for appointments? Why?

4. Who is more likely to be late for an appointment, a man or a woman? Why?

My Financial Career

STEPHEN LEACOCK

Stephen Leacock (1869–1944) was born in England but moved with his parents to Canada, where he remained for the rest of his life—except for a brief period during which he attended the University of Chicago and received a Ph.D. in economics and political science. A distinguished scholar, he became chairman of the Department of Economics and Political Science at McGill University in Montreal. Despite his scholarly achievements, he is best known for his satirical and humorous writing. Leacock wrote over three hundred essays, articles, and humorous pieces during his lifetime. In the preface to *Sunshine Sketches of a Little Town* (1912) he remarked: "Personally, I would sooner have written 'Alice in Wonderland' than the whole Encyclopaedia Britannica." The following selection, which contains some British and Canadian idioms and vocabulary and uses the English style of punctuation, illustrates his mixed national background.

WHEN I GO INTO A BANK I get rattled°. The clerks rattle me; the wickets° rattle me; the sight of the money rattles me; everything rattles me.

confused, nervous
bank tellers' windows

The moment I cross the threshold° of a bank and attempt to transact° business there, I become an irresponsible° idiot.

doorway, entrance
conduct / undependable, carefree

I knew this beforehand, but my salary had been raised to fifty dollars a month and I felt that the bank was the only place for it.

So I shambled° in and looked timidly° round at the clerks. I had an idea that a person about to* open an account must needs* consult the manager.

walked unsteadily, shuffled along / shyly, fearfully

I went up to a wicket marked 'Accountant.' The accountant was a tall, cool devil. The very sight of him rattled me. My voice was sepulchral°.

sad, solemn

'Can I see the manager?' I said, and added solemnly, 'alone.' I don't know why I said 'alone.'

'Certainly,' said the accountant, and fetched° him.

brought

The manager was a grave°, calm man. I held my fifty-six dollars clutched in a crumpled° ball in my pocket.

very serious
crushed together

'Are you the manager?' I said. God knows I didn't doubt it.

'Yes,' he said.

'Can I see you,' I asked, 'alone?' I didn't want to say 'alone' again, but without it the thing seemed self-evident°.

clear

The manager looked at me in some alarm°. He felt that I had an awful° secret to reveal.

fear
very bad, terrible

'Come in here,' he said, and led the way* to a private room. He turned the key in the lock.

'We are safe from interruption here,' he said: 'sit down.'

We both sat down and looked at each other. I found no voice to speak.

'You are one of Pinkerton's men*, I presume°,' he said.

suppose, assume

He had gathered° from my mysterious manner that I was a detective. I knew what he was thinking, and it made me worse.

'No, not from Pinkerton's,' I said, seeming to imply° that I came from a rival° agency.

'To tell the truth,' I went on, as if I had been prompted to lie about it, 'I am not a detective at all. I have come to open an account. I intend° to keep all my money in this bank.'

The manager looked relieved but still serious: he concluded now that I was a son of Baron Rothschild or a young Gould°.

'A large account, I suppose,' he said.

'Fairly large,' I whispered. 'I propose to deposit fifty-six dollars now and fifty dollars a month regularly.'

The manager got up and opened the door. He called to the accountant.

'Mr. Montgomery,' he said unkindly loud, 'this gentleman is opening an account, he will deposit fifty-six dollars. Good morning.'

I rose.

A big iron door stood open at the side of the room.

'Good morning,' I said, and stepped into the safe°.

'Come out,' said the manager coldly°, and showed me the other way.

I went up to the accountant's wicket and poked the ball of money at him with a quick convulsive° movement as if I were doing a conjuring° trick.

My face was ghastly° pale.

'Here,' I said, 'deposit it.' The tone of the words seemed to mean, 'Let us do this painful thing while the fit° is on us.'

He took the money and gave it to another clerk.

He made me write the sum on a slip and sign my name in a book. I no longer knew what I was doing. The bank swam before my eyes*.

'Is it deposited?' I asked in a hollow, vibrating voice.

'It is,' said the accountant.

'Then I want to draw a cheque*.'

My idea was to draw out* six dollars of it for present use. Someone gave me a cheque-book through a wicket and someone else began telling me how to write it out. The people in the bank had the impression that I was an invalid millionaire. I wrote something on the cheque and thrust° it in at the clerk. He looked at it.

'What! are you drawing it all out again?' he asked in surprise. Then I realized that I had written fifty-six instead of six. I was too far gone to reason now. I had a feeling it was impossible to explain the thing. All the clerks had stopped writing to look at me.

Glosses (right margin):
- got an idea or impression
- suggest
- competing
- plan
- an American millionaire
- safe
- in an unfriendly way
- violently shaking
- magical
- very; ghostly
- mood
- pushed with force

Reckless° with misery, I made a plunge*.   careless

'Yes, the whole thing.'

'You withdraw your money from the bank?'

'Every cent of it.'

'Are you not going to deposit any more?' said the clerk,
astonished°.   amazed, greatly surprised

'Never.'

An idiot° hope struck me that they might think something   foolish
had insulted me while I was writing the cheque and that I had
changed my mind. I made a wretched° attempt to look like a man   unsuccessful; miserable
with a fearfully° quick temper.   terribly; very great

The clerk prepared to pay the money.

'How will you have it?' he said.

'What?'

'How will you have it?'

'Oh'—I caught his meaning* and answered without even trying to think—'in fifties.'

He gave me a fifty-dollar bill.

'And the six?' he asked dryly.

'In sixes,' I said.

He gave it me and I rushed out.

As the big door swung behind me I caught the echo of a roar
of laughter that went up to the ceiling of the bank. Since then I
bank no more. I keep my money in cash in my trousers pocket
and my savings in silver dollars in a sock.

IDIOMS AND PHRASES*

about to	*ready to*
must needs	*has to*
led the way	*went before and showed the way, guided*
Pinkerton's men	*guards sent by a company that specializes in protecting banks*
swam before my eyes	*seemed to be moving round and round*
draw a cheque	*write a check*
draw out	*withdraw, take out*
made a plunge	*did something risky or difficult*
caught his meaning	*heard, understood*

A

COMPREHENSION QUESTIONS

1. Why did the hero want to open a bank account?

2. Why is the story called "My Financial Career"?

3. Is the hero of the story young or old? Defend your opinion.

4. Does the story actually state why he's afraid of banks? Can you give some reasons for his fear?

5. Can our hero find a safe place for his money other than in the bank?

6. Do you have a bank account? Is it a savings or a checking account? What are the differences?

B

VOCABULARY BUILDER

Replace the word under the blank with the word from the following list that is closest to it in meaning.

convulsive	irresponsible	presume	gather
thrust	shambled	threshold	grave
fearful	crumpled	fetched	awful
safe	intend	ghastly	astonished
self-evident	wretched	reckless	

1. She had a _____ problem to discuss with her teacher.
(terrible)

2. The solution was _____.
(clearly apparent)

3. The old man _____ in and sat down with difficulty.
(shuffled)

4. With a _____ and tearful face, the girl watched the train pull away.
(very serious)

5. People who spend more than they earn are said to be _____ about money.
(undependable)

6. Wipe your feet before you step over the _____ into the house.
(doorway, entrance)

7. The dog always ————————————— my slippers.
(got, brought)

8. All the sales slips were ————————————— in a heap on the desk.
(crushed together)

9. I ————————————— that you will attend the next meeting.
(suppose)

10. With a quick, ————————————— movement, the pickpocket ran into
(violent)
the crowd

11. Her face ————————————— pale, the young woman heard the news
(ghostly)
of her fiancé's death.

12. I don't ————————————— to go on living here for more than two
(plan)
years.

13. The ————————————— beggar stood shivering in the snow.
(miserable)

14. His strength ————————————— the onlookers at the circus.
(greatly surprised)

15. He ————————————— the stick into the ground with great
(pushed)
determination.

16. With ————————————— foolishness, she pressed hard on the gas
(careless)
pedal and sped off into the sunset.

17. The lion gave a ————————————— roar, and all the animals in the
(very great)
jungle scattered.

18. I ————————————— that you are here to apply for the job.
(get the idea)

19. Keep your valuables in a —————————————.
(vault)

C

IDIOMS

Fill in the blank with the correct phrase.

led the way   swam before my eyes   too far gone

1. The usher _____ to our seats.

2. The telegram _____ as I read about the terrible accident.

3. The drunk was _____ to walk a straight line.

4. The salesperson _____ to the fitting room.

5. The room _____ as my dizziness increased.

6. The gambler was _____ to stop.

D

WORD FORMS

Fill in the correct form of the words listed below.

1. interrupt, interrupted, interrupting, interruption

   a. He became annoyed at the _____.

   b. I hope I'm not _____ anything.

   c. Please don't _____ me when I'm speaking.

   d. John's sleep was rudely _____ by the ringing of the alarm clock.

2. doubt, doubted, doubting

   a. I _____ whether I can finish my homework on time.

   b. Because Mary is suspicious, she is always _____ everyone.

   c. There is no _____ in my mind that I shall do a good job.

   d. Because Ann had a very busy week planned, she _____ whether she would be able to see Tom during that time.

3. imply, implied, implying, implication

 a. By putting his hand over the letter, he _____ that he didn't want anyone to read it.

 b. I'm not trying to _____ anything.

 c. We wonder what the _____ of computers is for the future.

 d. Yesterday, David _____ he was very busy by describing his many activities.

4. swim, swam, swimmer, swimming

 a. _____ is healthy, invigorating, and enjoyable.

 b. You can see he is a good _____ .

 c. Yesterday, Marvin _____ ten laps in the swimming pool.

 d. Do you know how to _____?

5. intend, intended, intentions, intending

 a. Since I don't spend everything I earn, I _____ to deposit some money in the bank.

 b. Mr. Jones asked Alan, "What are your _____ concerning my daughter?"

 c. Ethel _____ to study, but she didn't have enough time.

 d. What are you _____ to do with the money you won?

E

SPELLING

Rewrite using the correct spelling.

1. Add -ing to the following words.

Examples: hit + ing = **hitting**   share + ing = **sharing**

a. stare + ing
b. presume + ing
c. rise + ing
d. snap + ing

e. sit + ing
f. fit + ing
g. write + ing
h. swim + ing

2. Give the plural form of the following words.

Example: story + s = **stories**

a. cookie + s
b. wife + s
c. misery + s
d. family + s
e. lady + s

f. knife + s
g. story + s
h. theory + s
i. valley + s
j. industry + s

F

MAKING MORE INTERESTING AND ECONOMICAL SENTENCES

Combine each of the following sets of sentences into one sentence.

Example: The clerks rattle me. The wickets rattle me. The sight of the money rattles me.

The clerks, wickets, and money rattle me.

1. I have come to open an account. I intend to keep all my money in this bank.

2. The manager got up and opened the door. He called to the accountant.

3. I was too far gone to reason now. I had a feeling it was impossible to explain the thing.

4. The bank lost the check. The clerk had made a mistake.

5. My check bounced. I had insufficient funds.

6. You may ask the teller for a check. You may ask the teller for cash.

7. You can deposit money in a bank. You can buy savings bonds from a bank.

8. All banks lend money. Some banks charge more interest than others.

9. Banks are safe. Each account is insured by the federal government.

10. You can withdraw money from your account. You cannot withdraw more money than you have in your account.

G

"IT'S" AND "ITS"

I. Fill in the correct form, either **it's** or **its.**

1. A checking account is very useful because _____ possible to withdraw money without going to the bank.

2. _____ incredible that such deposits can be handled so quickly.

3. A bank must take good care of _____ depositors.

4. What impressed me most about the play was _____ dry humor.

5. The problem with advice is that _____ usually unwanted.

6. Doctors often feel _____ important for their patients to get a yearly checkup.

7. _____ clear to see that the car is a great invention, although some people feel _____ disadvantages outweigh _____ advantages.

8. The organization held _____ convention in a small hotel.

9. The United States encourages _____ citizens to vote in every election.

10. _____ a wonder that the car didn't lose _____ muffler after hitting that pothole.

II. Write five of your own sentences using either **it's** or **its.**

H

ADJECTIVES

Write a paragraph using as many of the following adjectives as you can.

astonished   awful   timid
wretched   convulsive   reckless
grave

I

SUBJECT-VERB AGREEMENT

Choose the correct word from those in parentheses.

1. The woman as well as most of her children (speaks/speak) French.

2. I (want/wants) to buy a new dress.

3. Two members of the club (was/were) late today.

4. The company (have/has) decided to go out of business.

5. Each person with measles (has/have) been quarantined.

6. Both women (feel/feels) tired.

7. Each person in here (has/have) a ticket.

8. The girls and their friend (sleep/sleeps) in the spare room.

9. There (has/have) been several calls for you.

10. Neither he nor they (wish/wishes) to make trouble.

J

TOPICS FOR WRITING AND DISCUSSION

1. How do you make deposits and withdrawals at your bank?

2. Do people keep their money in banks only because banks are safe, or are there other advantages of banks? What are they?

3. What kinds of services does your bank offer its depositors? Any of the following?

Check-writing privileges
Savings bank life insurance
Safe-deposit boxes
Mortgages
Credit cards

4. Fill out the sample check and bank forms on pages 50 and 51.

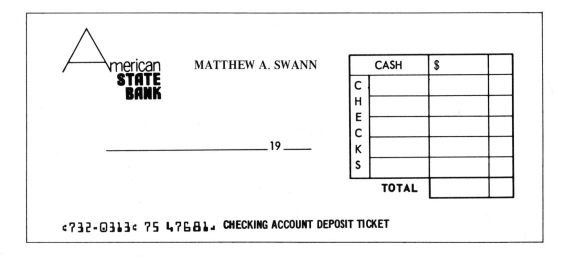

American STATE BANK

MATTHEW A. SWANN
18 Chelsea Place
New York, N.Y. 10011

NO. 159 _____ 19 _____

PAY TO THE ORDER OF _____ $ _____

_____ DOLLARS

⑆732-0313⑆ 75 47681⑈

American STATE BANK

MATTHEW A. SWANN

_____ 19 ___

CASH	$	
C		
H		
E		
C		
K		
S		
TOTAL		

⑆732-0313⑆ 75 47681⑈   CHECKING ACCOUNT DEPOSIT TICKET

MIDLAND BANK   **SAVINGS DEPOSIT**

PLEASE ENDORSE EACH CHECK	DOLLARS	CENTS
CASH		
COIN		
CHECKS AS FOLLOWS ON:		
TOTAL ▶		

_____OFFICE   DATE_____
DEPOSIT FOR THE ACCOUNT OF ▼

_____

_____

MY ACCOUNT NUMBER IS

DO NOT WRITE BELOW THIS LINE

MIDLAND BANK   **SAVINGS WITHDRAWAL**
                                                    NON-NEGOTIABLE

_____OFFICE   DATE_____

PAY THE SUM OF . . . . $_____

_____ DOLLARS

MY ACCOUNT NUMBER IS   TO:_____
                                                  ACCOUNT OWNER SIGNATURE

                                                  _____
                                                  ADDRESS

Old Country Advice to the
American Traveler

WILLIAM SAROYAN

William Saroyan (1908–   ) was born in Fresno, California, of Armenian parents. Known for his touching and sentimental stories praising personal freedom, America, and life in general, he has tried almost every kind of writing: short stories, plays, and novels. He first won fame with a collection of stories, *The Daring Young Man on the Flying Trapeze* (1934), and later with the play *The Time of Your Life* (1939), for which he was awarded—and refused to accept—the Pulitzer Prize in 1940. His first novel, *My Name Is Aram* (1940), reflected the experiences of growing up as an Armenian-American in California's San Joaquin Valley. Saroyan served in the army during World War II and returned to California, where he now lives. This selection is taken from *My Name Is Aram*, and the accompanying illustration is from the original edition of the book.

ONE YEAR MY UNCLE MELIK traveled from Fresno to New York. Before he got aboard the train his uncle Garro paid him a visit* and told him about the dangers of travel.

When you get on the train, the old man said, choose° your seat carefully, sit down, and do not look about*.   select

Yes, sir, my uncle said.

Several moments after the train begins to move, the old man said, two men wearing uniforms will come down the aisle and ask you for your ticket. Ignore them. They will be impostors°.   people pretending to be what they are not

How will I know? my uncle said.

You will know, the old man said. You are no longer a child.

Yes, sir, my uncle said.

Before you have traveled twenty miles an amiable° young man will come to you and offer you a cigarette. Tell him you don't smoke. The cigarette will be doped°.   friendly

full of a drug or narcotic

Yes, sir, said my uncle.

On your way to the diner a very beautiful young woman will bump into* you intentionally° and almost embrace you, the old man said. She will be extremely apologetic° and attractive° and your natural impulse° will be to cultivate° her friendship. Dismiss your natural impulse and go on in and eat. The woman will be an adventuress°.   on purpose
full of regrets / pretty
feeling / develop

woman who seeks to earn money dishonestly

A what? my uncle said.

A whore°, the old man shouted. Go on in and eat. Order the best food, and if the diner is crowded, and the beautiful young woman sits across the table from you, do not look into her eyes. If she speaks, pretend to be deaf°.   prostitute

unable to hear

Yes, sir, my uncle said.

Pretend to be deaf, the old man said. That is the only way out of it.*

Out of what? my uncle said.

Out of the whole ungodly° mess, the old man said. I have   shameful
traveled. I know what I'm talking about.

Yes, sir, my uncle said.

Let's say no more about it, the old man said.

Yes, sir, my uncle said.

Let's not speak of the matter again, the old man said. It's
finished. I have seven children. My life has been a full and right-
eous° one. Let's not give it another thought. I have land, vines,   just, godly
trees, cattle, and money. One cannot have everything—except for
a day or two at a time.

Yes, sir, my uncle said.

On your way back to your seat from the diner, the old man
said, you will pass through the smoker°. There you will find a   railway car in which
game of cards in progress*. The players will be three middle-aged   passengers may smoke
men with expensive-looking rings on their fingers. They will nod
at you pleasantly and one of them will invite you to join the
game. Tell them, No speak English.

Yes, sir, my uncle said.

That is all, the old man said.

Thank you very much, my uncle said.

One thing more, the old man said. When you go to bed at
night, take your money out of your pocket and put it in your shoe.
Put your shoe under your pillow, keep your head on the pillow all
night, *and don't sleep.*

Yes, sir, my uncle said.

That is all, the old man said.

The old man went away and the next day my uncle Melik got
aboard the train and traveled straight across America to New
York. The two men in uniforms were not impostors, the young
man with the doped cigarette did not arrive, the beautiful young
woman did not sit across the table from my uncle in the diner,
and there was no card game in progress in the smoker. My uncle
put his money in his shoe and put his shoe under his pillow and put
his head on the pillow and didn't sleep all night the first night, but
the second night he abandoned° the whole ritual°.   gave up, stopped / plan,
                                                                        ceremony

The second day he *himself* offered another young man a
cigarette which the other young man accepted. In the diner my
uncle went out of his way to sit at a table with a young lady. He
started a poker game in the smoker, and long before the train ever
got to New York my uncle knew everybody aboard° the train and   on, in
everybody knew him. Once, while the train was traveling through

Ohio, my uncle and the young man who had accepted the cigarette and two young ladies on their way to Vassar° formed a
quartette and sang *The Wabash Blues.*

a college in New York
State

The journey was a very pleasant one.

When my uncle Melik came back from New York, his old
uncle Garro visited him again.

I see you are looking all right, he said. Did you follow my
instructions?

Yes, sir, my uncle said.

The old man looked far away in space.

I am pleased that *someone* has profited by my experience, he
said.

IDIOMS AND PHRASES*

paid him a visit	*came to see him*
look about	*look all around*
bump into	*walk into*
way out of it	*solution (to the problem)*
in progress	*happening, going on*

A

COMPREHENSION QUESTIONS

1. What does Uncle Garro warn Melik
about?

2. Why does Uncle Garro warn him?

3. Did Melik follow Uncle Garro's advice?

4. Did Melik enjoy his train trip?

5. Would Melik have enjoyed it as much
if he had followed Uncle Garro's advice?
Why?

6. Can you explain the ending? Why does
Melik lie to Uncle Garro? Does Uncle
Garro believe him?

7. Do you think Uncle Garro followed his
own advice when he was young?

B

VOCABULARY BUILDER

Select the correct definition of the underlined word by circling **a**, **b**, **c**, or **d**.

1. We can find no way out of this <u>ungodly</u> mess.

   a. shameful   **c.** happy
   b. doubtful   **d.** gloomy

2. Some people go through a <u>ritual</u> before they retire to bed.

   a. shower   **c.** choice
   b. mess   **d.** routine

3. If you want to protect your reputation, you must <u>choose</u> your friends carefully.

   a. like   **c.** treat
   b. select   **d.** correct

4. He <u>abandoned</u> the idea because it wasn't practical.

   a. disliked   **c.** gave up
   b. fought against   **d.** approved

5. It seems that the school was being run by two people who were <u>impostors</u>.

   a. pretenders   **c.** teachers
   b. professionals   **d.** students

6. If you have a <u>righteous</u> cause, you must fight for it.

   a. bad   **c.** old-fashioned
   b. modern   **d.** just

7. "I didn't know the drink was <u>doped</u>," the blonde said as she fell to the floor.

   a. drugged   **c.** cloudy
   b. mixed   **d.** sour

8. "Do you mean that you doped this drink <u>intentionally</u>?"

   a. at night   **c.** without knowing
   b. careless   **d.** on purpose

9. He was <u>apologetic</u> about his late arrival.

    a. full of sympathy   **c.** full of excuses
    b. careless   **d.** lying

10. His first <u>impulse</u> was to say no, but then he thought it over and approved the plan.

    a. feeling   **c.** answer
    b. word   **d.** job

11. Let's <u>pay him a visit</u> at the hospital and try to cheer him up.

    a. buy him presents   **c.** read to him
    b. telephone him   **d.** go to see him

12. There was a medical conference <u>in progress</u> when we entered the hospital.

    a. in the room   **c.** in a circle
    b. happening   **d.** ending

13. The saleswoman behind the counter gave him an <u>amiable</u> smile as she handed him his package.

    a. lovely   **c.** friendly
    b. sweet   **d.** crooked

C

ADJECTIVES AND ADVERBS

Fill in the blanks with the correct word in parentheses.

    1. He was a _____ student. (well/good)

    2. He did his work _____. (well/good)

    3. I slept _____ last night. (well/good)

    4. She sang _____. (beautiful/beautifully)

    5. He was _____ about his profession. (serious/seriously)

    6. He took his profession _____. (serious/seriously)

    7. They left the room _____. (quiet/quietly)

8. The _____ class left the room _____.
(quiet/quietly)

9. She played tennis _____. (bad/badly)

10. Those shoes go _____ with your dress. (well/good)

11. He stopped the car _____. (short/shortly)

12. _____ thereafter, they were transferred to another
city. (short/shortly)

13. He did _____ in mathematics. (bad/badly)

14. He looked at him _____. (penetrating/penetratingly)

15. He gave him a _____ look. (penetrating/penetratingly)

16. He exhaled _____. (slow/slowly)

17. He was a _____ driver. (slow/slowly)

18. Drive _____. (slow/slowly)

19. She was _____ because her daughter was two hours
late. (frantic/frantically)

20. In the rain, she waved _____ for a taxi.
(frantic/frantically)

D

IMPERATIVES

When Uncle Garro gives advice, he often does so in imperative sentences. An imperative
sentence is one that issues a request or command or gives instructions.

1. **Let's (let us)** expresses the imperative in the first person. We use **let's (let us)** in
commands, requests, proposals, or suggestions in which the speaker includes
himself or herself.

Example: Let's (let us) leave the party.

Let's (let us) have fun elsewhere.

Rewrite the commands below using **let us** or **let's**.

   a. Study for the test.

   b. Meet me for lunch tomorrow.

   c. We will eat in the cafeteria.

   d. You and I will give him the information he wants.

   e. You and I will not give him the information he wants.

2. Read the story again and pick out all the imperative sentences you can find. Then make up eight sentences of your own following the patterns found in the story. For example:

Ignore them.
If she speaks, pretend to be deaf.

When you get on the train, choose your seat carefully.
Let's say no more about it.

E

COMBINING SENTENCES BY USING RELATIVE PRONOUNS

Combine the following sentences by using **that**, **which**, or **who**.

Examples: The man ran into the house. He was in a hurry.

   The man who was in a hurry ran into the house.

   The item was finally put on the agenda. We discussed it yesterday.
   The item that we discussed yesterday was finally put on the agenda.

   1. The tall man builds bridges. He is wearing a blue shirt.

   2. Jerry was standing at the corner. He saw the girl.

   3. Some examples of borrowed words are *café*, *garage*, and *menu*. These words were borrowed from French.

   4. Prefixes can be added to some words. This addition gives them different meanings.

   5. Some mushrooms are poisonous. They look very safe.

   6. The lovers were running down the street. They were holding hands.

   7. Jack and Jill went up the hill. They were carrying a pail of water.

   8. Give generously to the Red Cross. It is a good cause.

9. The woman attracted our attention. She was standing in the doorway.

10. The picture belongs to the art teacher. The picture is on the wall.

F

QUOTATION MARKS

As you may have noted, the story does not contain any quotation marks. In the following passage, put quotation marks where you think they are needed.

Let's say no more about it, the old man said.

Yes, sir, my uncle said.

Let's not speak of the matter again, the old man said. It's finished. I have seven children. My life has been a full and righteous one. Let's not give it another thought. I have land, vines, trees, cattle, and money. One cannot have everything—except for a day or two at a time.

Yes, sir, my uncle said.

On your way back to your seat from the diner, the old man said, you will pass through the smoker. There you will find a game of cards in progress. The players will be three middle-aged men with expensive-looking rings on their fingers. They will nod at you pleasantly and one of them will invite you to join the game. Tell them, No speak English.

Yes, sir, my uncle said.

That is all, the old man said.

Thank you very much, my uncle said.

One thing more, the old man said. When you go to bed at night, take your money out of your pocket and put it in your shoe. Put your shoe under your pillow, keep your head on the pillow all night, *and don't sleep.*

G

PREPOSITIONS OF TIME AND PLACE

Answer the following in complete sentences.

1. When did you arrive at school today?

2. What time did you leave your house?

3. When do you eat dinner?

4. When were you born?

5. Last summer, where did you go on vacation? For how long?

6. Where do you go shopping for groceries? When?

7. What countries have you traveled to?

8. Where is your school located?

9. Where do you live? Give the street, city, state, and country.

10. Give directions on how to get from your home to your school.

H

TOPICS FOR WRITING AND DISCUSSION

1. Compare airplane travel with train travel. Which do you prefer? Why?

2. Are the dangers of travel still the same as in Uncle Garro's time?

3. Tell about a long journey that you've taken. What were your most memorable adventures?

4. What travel advice do you have for young people?

This Year
It's Going to Be Different

WILL STANTON

Will Stanton (1918–) is a humorist and a magazine writer. He has published more than 150 articles in such magazines as *Reader's Digest*, *McCall's*, and *The New Yorker*. Some of his stories have been made into films; one of them is Walt Disney's *Charlie and the Angel*, which is based on a story from the collection *The Golden Evenings of Summer* (1971). The following story, retitled "Happy New Year, Mrs. Robinson," appears in his collection *The Old Familiar Booby Traps of Home* (1978).

NEW YEAR'S RESOLUTIONS* are like anything else—you get out of them what you put in. Judging from results other years, I had never put enough in, but this year was going to be different. I read books on self-improvement before I wrote my list. Find some beauty in everything. . . . Make the other fellow feel important. . . . About thirty like that. Pretty clearly, anyone who followed my collection of rules would be blessed with a richer life, boundless° love from his family, and the admiration of the community. I could hardly wait until New Year's Day.

    When I came downstairs Maggie, my wife, was at the kitchen sink. I tiptoed over and kissed her on the back of the neck. (Resolution No. 1: Be spontaneous° in showing affection.) She shrieked° and dropped a cup. "Don't ever sneak up* on me like that again!" she cried.

    "You're looking lovely this morning," I said. (A sincere compliment is worth its weight in gold*.)

    "Look," she said, "it wasn't my idea to stay out until four a.m."

    I took some aspirin and coffee into the living room. I'd just started reading the paper when Sammy, our five-year-old, came in. He was wearing the watch he'd received for Christmas. "Say, Dad," he said, "what makes a watch run°?"

    In the old days* I would have told him to ask his mother. Instead, I got a pencil and drew a sketch° of the escapement mechanism°. (Always encourage your child's curiosity.) It took about fifteen minutes, and Sammy wandered off several times, but I kept calling him back. "There," I said, "that's what makes your watch run."

    "Then how come* it doesn't?" he asked.

    His brother Roy walked by. "You have to wind° it," said Roy. Sammy wound it and held it to his ear. He smiled. "Roy sure is smart," he said.

    Our daughter Gretchen came in with her doll, Mrs. Robinson. "Good morning, Gretchen," I said. "Happy New Year, Mrs. Robinson." (Meet your child at his own level.)

unlimited

unplanned, natural
made a loud cry

operate

drawing, diagram

turn the crown to tighten
the spring mechanism

"It isn't either happy," said Gretchen. "Mrs. Robinson is sick. Probably a coronary°."   — heart attack

"Why don't you take her to see Dr. Sammy?" I suggested. "He can use his new doctor's kit°."   — set of instruments

The phone rang, and I answered it. It was a friend of our daughter Kit. "Happy New Year, Marilyn," I said. "What have you been doing over the holidays?" (Show an interest in your children's friends.) She said she hadn't been doing anything much. "Come now, a pretty girl like you," I said jovially°—"I'll bet the fellows are swarming° around. . . . What's that? Yes, of course you can speak to Kit. Certainly."   — merrily / crowding

Kit was in her room with the record player going very loud. I rapped° on the door. She called out something, and I went in. She was in her pajamas. "I didn't say you could come in!" she yelled, grabbing° a robe and holding it in front of her. At fourteen, she has become extremely° aware of being female.   — knocked loudly / taking suddenly / greatly, very

"I'm sorry. I couldn't understand you," I said apologetically. To ease the situation*, I picked up her brand-new° sweater from the floor and put it over a chair.   — newly purchased

"I was going to pick it up," she said defensively°. "You don't always put *your* things away."   — protectively

There was a series° of shrieks down the hall. I found Gretchen in tears. Roy and Sammy were about to* perform open-heart surgery on Mrs. Robinson with a scout knife°. "She told us Mrs. Robinson was sick," Roy said.   — an orderly arrangement

I suggested that they carve° something for their mother—like a salad spoon. (Encourage creativity° in the young.)   — cut into a shape with a knife / artistic expression

In the kitchen, Maggie wanted to know what was wrong with Gretchen. "Mrs. Robinson had a coronary," I told her.

"I know you're not feeling your best after last night," she said, "but I'm getting a little tired of these smart° remarks. Would you mind taking the garbage out?"   — rude, disrespectful

"I'd be happy to," I said. (The most trivial° chore can prove rewarding if approached with zest°.)   — unimportant / sharp enjoyment

"Do you have to be so sarcastic°." she said.   — bitter, nasty

It seemed that my resolutions weren't working the way the books had said. I didn't quit, though. I helped the boys build a

escapement
mechanism

scout knife

snowman—only Sammy got his feet wet and Roy lost his mittens and they went inside. I played jacks° with Gretchen, but she said I didn't do it right. I struck up* a conversation with Kit, trying to establish some kind of rapport°. I touched on* hippies, pop music, dating, morality and so on. She contributed very little. Anybody else would have thrown in the sponge*, but I kept trying. For example, Maggie always dreads° taking down the Christmas tree, so I thought I'd do it for her. (Take over one of your wife's chores°, she'll love you for it.)

    I was about two thirds done° when Maggie came in. "Oh, no!" she cried. "I wanted it left up for the party tonight. Can't you just sit and watch a football game? Please? It's what you usually do on New Year's."

    "This year is different," I said.

    "Yes, isn't it?" She shook her head. "I swear I don't know. The kids have been impossible all day. I found the boys whittling° on my best salad spoon, and then they had the nerve° to say you suggested it. And Kit has been in a poisonous° mood. She said that Marilyn phoned and you didn't tell her. And that you cross-examined° Marilyn about her boyfriends."

    "Hold it!" I said. "I was only making small talk*." By now the kids were in the room, drawn° by the commotion°.

    "You never bothered with small talk before. Why start now?"

    "Because it's New Year's," I said. I explained to the assembled gathering about the books and the resolutions and what I'd been trying to accomplish. Silence. The kids stood there looking uneasily° at each other. "A man wants to improve himself," I said. "He wants to be a better husband, a better father—"

    "We all want to be better," Maggie said. "Except that when you're so considerate° it doesn't seem natural. If the kids do something and you get mad, they know where they stand*. But when you're so even-tempered°—"

    "Yeah," Kit said. "You didn't say a word about my clothes on the floor. You just smiled. It made me sick."

    Roy said, "I been° in more trouble today. . . ."

    Gretchen said, "I think it was better when you didn't play jacks."

    "And yelled," Sammy said, "and said 'damitall°.'"

    "All right," I snarled°. "I make every effort* to be a good father, and this is the thanks I get. The fact is, you don't deserve the father you've got."

    I was illustrating my points with gestures. "You're the ones who'd better start making resolutions. Like doing your homework, cleaning your rooms, letting the spoons alone. And when I tell you to do something, jump!"

Marginal glosses:

a children's game

agreement, harmony

fears greatly

small jobs

finished (past tense of did)

shaping wood with a knife / impoliteness; boldness / harmful

questioned closely

attracted / great noise

uncomfortably

thoughtful of others

calm

incorrect English

damn it all—mild curse
growled angrily

I reached out to steady° a lamp I had brushed with my sleeve. make stable
"Furthermore°—" At this moment, I realized suddenly that the also
atmosphere had changed. The kids were sprawled° on the floor, resting carelessly
relaxed. I turned to Maggie.

"Why is everybody smiling? What's the big joke?"

"No joke," she said. "We're just happy to have you back again."

IDIOMS AND PHRASES*

New Year's resolutions	*promises made at New Year's to improve or reform*
sneak up	*come slowly and unnoticed*
worth its weight in gold	*very valuable*
old days	*long ago*
how come	*why*
ease the situation	*make things less tense*
about to	*ready to*
struck up	*began, started*
touched on	*spoke of briefly, mentioned*
thrown in the sponge	*admitted defeat*
making small talk	*talking about unimportant matters*
know where they stand	*know their position in the relationship*
make every effort	*do one's best*

A

COMPREHENSION QUESTIONS

1. What was our hero going to do differently this year?

2. How did Maggie, his wife, react to his show of affection?

3. How did Sammy get his watch to run? Why did he lose patience with his father?

4. How did Gretchen's brothers plan to heal her doll?

5. How did our hero show an interest in Kit's friend?

6. What was Kit's reaction to her father's picking up her clothes?

7. How was Mrs. Robinson saved from open-heart surgery?

8. Name four things our hero did to be friendly and helpful to his family.

9. Why was the family unhappy with our hero's behavior?

10. Why do people make New Year's resolutions?

B

VOCABULARY BUILDER

I. Find the synonym in the second column that best matches the word or phrase in the first column.

1. odd jobs in the home	**a.** sprawled
2. understanding	**b.** rapport
3. heart attack	**c.** rapped
4. knocked loudly	**d.** coronary
5. yelled loudly	**e.** shrieked
6. determination or promise to improve	**f.** carve
7. drawing	**g.** sketch
8. crowding around	**h.** resolution
9. cut into a shape	**i.** swarming
10. spread out	**j.** chores

II. Jane and Mary have different personalities. Whatever Jane does, says, or is, Mary is completely the opposite. From the following descriptions of Jane, supply the opposite qualities (antonyms) for Mary. Choose from this list:

boundless	trivial	drawn by
spontaneous	sarcastic	considerate
smart	dreads	makes every effort
jovially		

1. Jane has limited energy. Mary's energy is ——————————————.

2. Jane is very sweet. Mary is often ————————————.

3. Jane always plans ahead. Mary is ————————————.

4. Jane lets only important things bother her, but Mary often makes a fuss over

—————————————— matters.

5. Jane looks forward to meeting new people, but Mary always ——————————— these meetings.

6. Mary sometimes gives ——————————— answers, but Jane is always respectful.

7. Jane generally fears any kind of danger, but Mary is always _____ the excitement.

8. Jane is sometimes tactless and rude, but Mary is always _____.

9. Jane will usually answer the telephone sadly, but Mary will always answer it

_____.

10. One girl always _____ to keep her New Year's resolutions, the other girl never makes them.

C

IDIOMS

Write your own sentences using each of the idiomatic expressions listed below.

Example: sneak up on

Please try not to sneak up on me, because it frightens me.

1. brand-new
2. throw in the sponge
3. cross-examined
4. worth its weight in gold
5. struck up

6. in the old days
7. touched on
8. ease the situation
9. making small talk
10. wander off

D

WORD FORMS

Fill in the correct form of the words listed below.

1. dread, dreading, dreadful

a. He was _____ the test.

b. The new hat looked _____.

c. I always _____ going to the dentist.

2. spontaneous, spontaneously, spontaneity

    a. Children show a great deal of ————————————————————— when
they play.

    b. There was ————————————————— applause when the movie
star entered the restaurant.

    c. Everyone responds ————————————————— to a smile.

3. perform, performed, performing, performance

    a. The doctor ————————————————— complicated surgery
yesterday.

    b. Will you ————————————————— for the class today?

    c. The ————————————————— was very amusing.

    d. The actors were ————————————————— before a very young
audience.

4. play, playing, player

    a. Were you ————————————————— cards last night?

    b. He is a very good chess —————————————————.

    c. ————————————————— the piano softly, please.

5. consider, considerate, considering, consideration

    a. He was ————————————————— whether to accept the job.

    b. He was a ————————————————— host.

    c. Do you ————————————————— him a kind person?

    d. The teacher showed no ————————————————— for her
students' needs.

E

PRESENT PERFECT TENSE

The present perfect tense is used for an action that began in the past and continues in the present. When we use the present perfect, we do not say precisely when the action took place. In the following sentences, supply the correct tense—simple past, past perfect, or present perfect—of the verb in parentheses.

Examples: Kit _____ in a bad mood yesterday.
(be)
Kit <u>was</u> in a bad mood yesterday.

For the past three days Kit _____ in a bad
(be)
mood.

For the past three days Kit <u>has been</u> in a bad mood.

1. This class _____ English for two months.
(study)

2. Last week I _____ a new dress for the party.
(buy)

3. Michael _____ as an engineer from 1973 to
(work)
1975.

4. Her father _____ on the door for the past
(rap)
ten minutes.

5. While he was winding his watch, he _____
(drop)
and _____ it.
(break)

6. He _____ his watch twice before.
(break)

7. I _____ my New Year's resolution to
(never keep)
be neat.

8. When she entered the room, he _____ to
(begin)
cry.

9. Ann now lives in Paris, where she _____
(live)
for five years.

10. John _____ his grandmother many times.
  (visit)

11. On Tuesday I _____ my notebook, and
  (lose)

  I _____ it yet.
  (not find)

12. At fifteen, she _____ extremely fashionable.
  (become)

13. What _____ you
  (have)

  _____ to improving your home?
  (contribute)

14. Before Allen came to New York, he _____
  (live)

  in Geneva.

15. The teacher _____ that same lecture many
  (give)

  times.

16. The weather _____ cold last winter.
  (be)

17. I _____ English since 1975.
  (study)

18. Judging by past test results, I _____
  (never study)

  enough.

19. I _____ just _____
  (have)   (start)

  reading the newspaper when my son _____ into the room.
  (come)

20. He _____ the tie he _____
  (wear)   (receive)

  for his birthday.

F

SENTENCE COMBINING

Combine the sentences below by following the suggested patterns.

1. I read books on self-improvement. I wrote my list.

  Before _____, I read _____

  _____.

2. Maggie is my wife. She was at the sink. I came downstairs.

Maggie, my _____, _____

when _____.

3. I'd started reading the paper. Sammy came in. Sammy is our five-year-old son.

I'd started _____ when Sammy, our

_____, _____.

4. He was wearing a watch. He had received a watch for Christmas.

He _____ that _____.

5. I struck up a conversation with Kit. I was trying to establish some kind of rapport.

In order to _____, I struck up

_____.

6.– 10. Make up your own five sentences, using each of the above patterns.

G

TOPICS FOR WRITING AND DISCUSSION

1. What kinds of New Year's resolutions would you make?

2. Have you ever kept a New Year's resolution? What was it?

3. Have your efforts to act nicer ever been misunderstood or misinterpreted?

4. What kinds of New Year's resolutions would you like your parents to make? Your teachers? Your friends?

5. Write a paragraph describing how you would go about keeping your New Year's resolutions.

A Bird in Hand–What's It Worth?

ELAINE HART MESSMER

Elaine Hart Messmer is a free-lance writer and a housewife. She has contributed to many magazines and collections of short stories. This selection is taken from *The Bedside Phoenix Nest* (1965), edited by Martin Levin.

WHEN YOUR OWN BACKYARD° is smack-up° against the city of Washington, D.C., as ours is, it's pretty hard to keep from wondering what's happening on the other side of the fence°, and especially behind the impressive doors of the magnificent mansions° along Embassy Row°. Yet, in two decades of living almost next door to all these foreign dignitaries°, I'd never met any of them to speak of, or to, with the exception of one time when my car locked bumpers° with that of a Far Eastern gentleman in a race for the same parking place.

piece of land behind a house / directly, exactly

barrier of wood or wire / grand houses / street where foreign embassies are located / important people

It wasn't until one day over lunch in a Chinese restaurant that I got the courage to do anything about this omission°. My fortune cookie° produced a slip of paper upon which was written, "Take what you've got and never want more."

lack, exclusion

I called the Chinese Embassy and asked the young lady who answered exactly what that meant. Did they really have such a proverb°? She replied, between giggles°, that the fortune cookie didn't lie; it was indeed an old Chinese proverb, and similar in meaning to our "A bird in the hand is worth two in the bush*." I told her I was so glad that we had something in common* and thanked her. She told me to "call any time."

saying / fits of laughter

It was then that I decided to find out if the rest of the world had this proverb in common with us. It would be a start, anyway, in neighborly° relations.

friendly

I had no trouble in my quest° at the Spanish Embassy. When I asked for the Spanish version of "A bird, etc.," the bright but highly amused young woman came up immediately with, "*Más vale pájaro en mano que cien volando.*" Any Spaniard knows that that means "Better to have one in hand than a hundred flying."

search

On to Nepal. With all they've got to worry about these days,

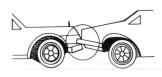

bumpers

fortune cookie

maybe they'd welcome a little cheerful diversion°. I was glad I
called. Not at first, but later on. I explained my mission to the
first woman who answered. She asked *"Who is this?"* and then,
"Whom are you with?" Finally, I managed to convince her that I
wasn't some gung-ho° ornithologist° who was flying high* and she
turned me over to another woman. In tones ringing on the highest
decibels° of annoyance°, she demanded another full explanation
and then deposited the entire problem in the lap of a pleasant,
cordial gentleman who *did* sound as though this might be the
brightest spot in his day. He told me that Nepal assuredly° did
have such a proverb, and did I want it in Nepalese? I told him that
English would do, and he informed me that in Nepal the prudent°
folk say, "A blind maternal° uncle is better than none at all."

 Well, I knew all this international good will was too good to
last, because I really came up against it* at the French Embassy.
The woman to whom I addressed my question about "A bird,
etc." was extremely excitable and gave me a verbal blast* in
rapid-fire° French. We parted on questionable terms.

 After the French debacle°, I turned north to Scandinavia,
where tempers are cooler. They are all pretty much in accord* and
claim that "A bird in the hand is worth two in the woods . . . or
on the roof . . . or in the tree." Take your pick*.

 The folk° in Iraq and the Somali Republic, although not
exactly Scandinavians, have the same proverb.

 A very courteous° lady at the German Embassy told me that
in Germany they feel that "The sparrow° in the hand is better
than the pigeon° on the roof."

 The Japanese say that it would be better not to pursue° two
rabbits when you already have one in your hand, or you may lose
all.

 At the Embassy of Ireland, a charming gentleman with one of
those O-apostrophe names felt that "sure the great wealth of Irish
culture could produce a similar proverb." He took my number
and called back the following morning to tell me that in Ireland
"A trout° in the hand is better than a salmon° in the pool."

 Next I called Greece. I was jostled° upward through the chain
of command* to a gentleman of cultural substance°. In Greece, he
told me, they say, "It's better to have one thing in your hand than
to wait for two."

 I really felt sorry for the poor man with whom I talked at the
Italian Embassy. He had to compete with a pneumatic drill° in
the background, as he tried with members of his staff to get to the
bottom* of the Italian version of the proverb. First, there were two
voices in excited Italian discussion, then three voices, then four.

Right column glosses:

change, distraction

(slang) foolishly
 enthusiastic / one
 who studies birds /
 units of sound / anger

certainly

wise
related through one's
 mother

fast
catastrophe

people

polite
a type of small bird
a grayish bird seen
 mostly in cities / run
 after

a type of small fish / a
 type of larger fish /
 pushed / content

pneumatic
 drill

Just about the time I was ready to give up*, he returned to the phone and shouted in triumph: "Better an egg today than a chicken tomorrow."

Russia must be accounted for, so I called the Soviet Embassy and put it to them straight*: Is there anything behind the Iron Curtain* to equal "A bird in the hand is worth two in the bush"? Consternation° threaded its way* through the wires. Did they consider this just one more U.S. achievement to top°? And I could just imagine my entire conversation being properly recorded, translated, computed, and rushed to the decoding room.

alarm
do better than

An eternity° later, the clerk came back to ask me, "How you say cuckoo° in English?"

a long time (without end)
a type of small bird

Finally, she returned again with the information that "The cuckoo in hand is worth more than the crane° in the sky." She seemed relieved that she'd been able to come up with* an answer for me.

a type of large bird

I am still puzzled by the Turkish Embassy. I talked with three different people there, ending with a gentleman who said, "*Yes, we do* have such a proverb!" There followed alternate periods of silence and hilarity° before he choked out, "I can't think of it!"

loud and constant laughter

And thus a day of neighborly relations came to an end.

IDIOMS AND PHRASES*

a bird in the hand is worth two in the bush	*don't risk what you have by trying to get what you don't have*
in common	*shared*
flying high	*very happy*
came up against	*faced a great difficulty*
verbal blast	*a strong, sudden rush of words*
in accord	*in agreement*
take your pick	*choose one*
chain of command	*different levels of authority in an organization, usually the military*
get to the bottom	*find the truth*
give up	*stop trying*
put it to them straight	*told them directly*
Iron Curtain	*Eastern European Communist countries*
threaded its way	*passed*
come up with	*provide*

A

COMPREHENSION QUESTIONS

1. Where does the author live?

2. Whom does she call to ask about a country's proverbs?

3. Name some of the embassies that refused to cooperate with her. Why?

4. How did the author become interested in the topic?

5. Do all the proverbs that the author learns have to do with birds?

6. Does the different way each embassy answers show something about that country?

B

VOCABULARY BUILDER

I. Answer yes or no to each of the following questions. Give reasons for your answers.

1. When your words cause <u>consternation</u> at a party, do you become the center of attention? Why?

2. At that same party, when someone <u>jostles</u> you, do you spill your drink?

3. If there is no <u>substance</u> to your story, do people call you a liar?

4. If you and your companion are in <u>accord</u>, are you quarreling?

5. If no one comes to your party, do you consider it a <u>debacle</u>?

6. If you speak <u>rapid-fire</u> English to a visiting Frenchman, will he understand you clearly?

7. Is it <u>prudent</u> to invite people who don't like each other to your party?

8. Are you better off inviting people who have something <u>in common</u>?

9. When someone tells you that <u>assuredly</u> he will come to your party, do you invite someone else instead?

10. If your guests are <u>gung-ho</u> for television, do you let them <u>turn on</u> the set?

11. Can you think of a better <u>diversion</u> for your party guests?

12. Do you do anything when the children at your party have the <u>giggles</u>?

13. Did you ever have any local <u>dignitaries</u> at your party?

14. Did an important <u>omission</u> from your guest list ever cause you embarrassment?

15. Does the <u>quest</u> for more original party games ever <u>bother</u> you?

II. Study your dictionary and then describe, in your own words, the following terms.

1. backyard
2. mansion

3. fortune cookie
4. bumpers

5. pneumatic drill

C

"WHO" AND "WHOM"

I. Fill in the blanks with **who** or **whom.**

Examples: _____ is this?   _____ are you with?

     Who is this?   **Whom are you with?**

     To_____ were you speaking?

     To whom were you speaking?

1. _____ is going to speak to the teacher?

2. To _____ is Miss Jones going to send a letter?

3. _____ drove you home from the embassy party?

4. _____ answered the telephone at your office?

5. To _____ did you send the book?

6. With _____ did your friends go to the theater?

7. _____ is considering your application for a job?

8. _____ is the woman to_____ I have to send the package?

9. With _____ does the United States have treaties?

10. _____ threw out my important papers?

11. For _____ did I bake this cake?

12. With _____ should I go to the party?

13. By _____ were you given the right to leave the country?

14. _____ were you talking to?

15. _____ do you have to meet on Friday?

D

PROVERBS

In your native language, give the expressions that have approximately the same meaning as the proverbs below. Translate your expressions into English.

1. Too many cooks spoil the broth.

2. The way to a man's heart is through his stomach.

3. Birds of a feather flock together.

4. A penny saved is a penny earned.

5. Time and tide wait for no man.

6. People in glass houses shouldn't throw stones.

7. A fool and his money are soon parted.

8. An ounce of prevention is worth a pound of cure.

9. The early bird catches the worm.

10. Familiarity breeds contempt.

11. You can catch more flies with honey than with vinegar.

12. It is not only fine feathers that make fine birds.

13. Do not count your chickens until they are hatched.

14. Strike while the iron is hot.

15. Do not put all your eggs in one basket.

E

NATIONALITIES AND LANGUAGES

Fill in the nationality and language for each of the countries listed below. For example, a person who lives in **Spain** is a **Spaniard,** and the language he or she speaks is **Spanish.**

1. Spain   **Spaniard**   **Spanish**

2. China   _____   _____

3. France   _____   _____

4. Iraq   _____   _____

5. Sweden _____   _____

6. Norway _____   _____

7. Greece _____   _____

8. Holland _____   _____

9. Nepal _____   _____

10. Germany _____   _____

11. Denmark _____   _____

12. England _____   _____

13. Russia _____   _____

14. Japan _____   _____

15. Italy _____   _____

16. Scotland _____   _____

17. Ireland _____   _____

18. Poland _____   _____

19. Hungary _____   _____

20. Turkey _____   _____

21. Israel _____   _____

F

TOPICS FOR WRITING AND DISCUSSION

1. Are proverbs always true? Can you think of some that are not?

2. The authors of most proverbs are unknown. Some come from works of literature by such famous authors as Shakespeare or Aesop. For fun, try to make up your own proverbs on the subjects of sleep, food, and friendship.

You Were Perfectly Fine

DOROTHY PARKER

Dorothy Parker (1893–1967) was an American journalist and short-story writer, in addition to being the author of a best-selling book of light verse. Many of her poems and light sketches first appeared in *The New Yorker*. Her books include *Enough Rope* (1926) and *Not So Deep a Well* (1933). Parker is most closely associated with the clever twenties and the Jazz Era. Many of her expressions and idioms come from that period when everyone was supposed to be carefree and gay and very clever. The humor in the following story is not always apparent, for the writer uses irony to make her point — everything she says is meant to be read in another way. Thus "you were perfectly fine" really means "you were awful." Read the story for such ironic meanings, and overlook some of the outdated idioms and slang expressions.

THE PALE YOUNG MAN eased° himself carefully into the low chair, and rolled his head to the side, so that the cool chintz° comforted his cheek and temple°.

"Oh, dear," he said. "Oh, dear, oh, dear, oh, dear. Oh."

The clear-eyed girl, sitting light and erect° on the couch, smiled brightly at him.

"Not feeling so well today?" she said.

"Oh, I'm great," he said. "Corking°, I am. Know what time I got up? Four o'clock this afternoon, sharp. I kept trying to make it, and every time I took my head off the pillow, it would roll under the bed. This isn't my head I've got on now. I think this is something that used to belong to Walt Whitman°. Oh, dear, oh, dear, oh, dear."

"Do you think maybe a drink would make you feel better?" she said.

"The hair of the mastiff that bit me*?" he said. "Oh, no, thank you. Please never speak of anything like that again. I'm through. I'm all, all through. Look at that hand; steady as a hummingbird°. Tell me, was I very terrible last night?"

"Oh, goodness," she said, "everybody was feeling pretty high°. You were all right."

"Yeah," he said. "I must have been dandy°. Is everybody sore° at me?"

"Good heavens, no," she said. "Everyone thought you were terribly funny. Of course, Jim Pierson was a little stuffy°, there, for a minute at dinner. But people sort of held him back in his chair, and got him calmed down. I don't think anybody at the other tables noticed at all. Hardly anybody."

"He was going to sock° me?" he said. "Oh, Lord. What did I do to him?"

"Why, you didn't do a thing," she said. "You were perfectly

Margin glosses:
eased° — moved slowly
chintz° — a glazed cotton material / temple° — side of the forehead
erect° — upright
Corking° — very good, excellent
Walt Whitman° — famous nineteenth-century American poet
hummingbird° — bird that makes a humming noise by the constant motion of its wings / high° — drunk / dandy° — wonderful / sore° — angry
stuffy° — old-fashioned
sock° — strike with force

fine. But you know how silly° Jim gets, when he thinks anybody is making too much fuss over Elinor."

"Was I making a pass at* Elinor?" he said. "Did I do that?"

"Of course you didn't," she said. "You were only fooling°, that's all. She thought you were awfully amusing. She was having a marvelous time. She only got a little tiny bit annoyed° just once, when you poured the clam-juice down her back."

"My God," he said. "Clam-juice down that back. And every vertebra° a little Cabot°. Dear God. What'll I ever do?"

"Oh, she'll be all right," she said. "Just send her some flowers, or something. Don't worry about it. It isn't anything."

"No, I won't worry," he said. "I haven't got a care° in the world. I'm sitting pretty*. Oh, dear, oh, dear. Did I do any other fascinating tricks at dinner?"

"You were fine," she said. "Don't be so foolish about it. Everybody was crazy about you. The maître d'hôtel was a little worried because you wouldn't stop singing, but he really didn't mind. All he said was, he was afraid they'd close the place again, if there was so much noise. But he didn't care a bit, himself. I think he loved seeing you have such a good time. Oh, you were just singing away, there, for about an hour. It wasn't so terribly loud, at all."

"So I sang," he said. "That must have been a treat°. I sang."

"Don't you remember?" she said. "You just sang one song after another. Everybody in the place was listening. They loved it. Only you kept insisting that you wanted to sing some song about some kind of fusiliers° or other, and everybody kept shushing you, and you'd keep trying to start it again. You were wonderful. We were all trying to make you stop singing for a minute, and eat something, but you wouldn't hear of it*. My, you were funny."

"Didn't I eat my dinner?" he said.

"Oh, not a thing," she said. "Every time the waiter would offer you something, you'd give it right back to him, because you said that he was your long-lost brother, changed in the cradle° by a gypsy band*, and that anything you had was his. You had him simply roaring° at you."

"I bet I did," he said. "I bet I was comical. Society's Pet. I must have been. And what happened then, after my overwhelming° success with the waiter?"

"Why, nothing much," she said. "You took a sort of dislike to some old man with white hair, sitting across the room, because you didn't like his necktie and you wanted to tell him about it. But we got you out, before he got really mad."

"Oh, we got out," he said. "Did I walk?"

foolish

joking

angry

part of the spinal column / aristocratic family in Massachusetts

a worry

a delight, something that gives great pleasure

old-fashioned infantry soldiers

infant's bed

shouting loudly (like a lion)

overpowering

"Walk! Of course you did," she said. "You were absolutely all right. There was that nasty° stretch° of ice on the sidewalk, and you did sit down awfully hard, you poor dear. But good heavens, that might have happened to anybody."

unpleasant / piece, unbroken length

"Oh, sure," he said. "Louisa Alcott° or anybody. So I fell down on the sidewalk. That would explain what's the matter with my—Yes. I see. And then what, if you don't mind?"

famous author of children's books

"Ah, now, Peter!" she said. "You can't sit there and say you don't remember what happened after that! I did think that maybe you were just a little tight° at dinner—oh, you were perfectly all right, and all that, but I did know you were feeling pretty gay. But you were so serious, from the time you fell down—I never knew you to be that way. Don't you know, how you told me I had never seen your real self before? Oh, Peter, I just couldn't bear it, if you didn't remember that lovely long ride we took together in the taxi! Please, you do remember that, don't you? I think it would simply kill me, if you didn't."

drunk

"Oh, yes," he said. "Riding in the taxi. Oh, yes, sure. Pretty long ride, hmm?"

"Round and round and round the park," she said. "Oh, and the trees were shining so in the moonlight. And you said you never knew before that you really had a soul."

"Yes," he said. "I said that. That was me."

"You said such lovely, lovely things," she said. "And I'd never known, all this time, how you had been feeling about me, and I'd never dared to let you see how I felt about you. And then last night—oh, Peter dear, I think that taxi ride was the most important thing that ever happened to us in our lives."

"Yes," he said. "I guess it must have been."

"And we're going to be so happy," she said. "Oh, I just want to tell everybody! But I don't know—I think maybe it would be sweeter to keep it all to ourselves*."

"I think it would be," he said.

"Isn't it lovely?" she said.

"Yes," he said. "Great."

"Lovely!" she said.

"Look here," he said, "do you mind if I have a drink? I mean, just medicinally°, you know. I'm off the stuff* for life, so help me. But I think I feel a collapse° coming on."

for reasons of health

breakdown, loss of physical strength

"Oh, I think it would do you good," she said. "You poor boy, it's a shame you feel so awful. I'll go make you a whisky and soda."

"Honestly," he said, "I don't see how you could ever want to speak to me again, after I made such a fool of myself, last night. I think I'd better go join a monastery° in Tibet."

"You crazy idiot!" she said. "As if I could ever let you go away now! Stop talking like that. You were perfectly fine."

She jumped up from the couch, kissed him quickly on the forehead, and ran out of the room.

The pale young man looked after her and shook his head long and slowly, then dropped it in his damp and trembling hands.

"Oh, dear," he said. "Oh, dear, oh, dear, oh, dear."

an isolated religious home for Buddhists, here suggesting a place that is very far away from the world

IDIOMS AND PHRASES*

the hair of the mastiff (dog) that bit me	*meaning here the same thing that hurt me*
making a pass at	*flirting with*
I'm sitting pretty	*all is well with me*
hear of it	*allow or consider it*
gypsy band	*roaming group*
keep it all to ourselves	*keep it secret*
off the stuff	*doing without it*

A

COMPREHENSION QUESTIONS

1. Was Peter really "perfectly fine"? Why not?

2. Why doesn't Peter remember anything?

3. Why didn't Peter eat anything? Was the waiter pleased with him?

4. Why was Jim Pierson angry with Peter?

5. What outrageous things did our hero do while he was drunk?

6. Did Peter (our hero) really want to marry the girl? How do you know?

B

VOCABULARY BUILDER

Fill in the blanks with words or phrases from the vocabulary list below.

chintz	dandy	a care
temple	sore	stretch
corking	stuffy	collapse
mastiff	nasty	I'm sitting pretty
overwhelming	sock	treat
keep it to ourselves	making a pass at	fusiliers
humming bird	vertebra	monastery
wouldn't hear of it	tight	

1. John was so upset after the fight with his girlfriend that he threatened to join a

_____.

2. His drinking had made him _____;
he couldn't walk a straight line.

3. Mother decided to give Nancy a _____,
so she took her to the circus.

4. Because Frank was under so much pressure, his doctors feared he would have a

nervous _____.

5. That _____ of road was so full of
potholes the car almost fell apart.

6. "Whew! That was a _____ bump,"
she said as she finally managed to get the car back on the road.

7. "I have an _____ desire to leave,"
he said. "This is a boring party."

8. "That's because the people here are so dull and _____,"
she said.

9. "I hope the hostess won't be _____
about our leaving," she said.

10. "Don't worry. I'll call her tomorrow and tell her we had a _____ good time."

11. "My goodness, it's hot in here," he said, wiping his _____ with a handkerchief.

12. "That _____ is growling very loudly. I wonder if he bites."

13. "If he jumps at you, I'll just _____ him."

14. "That's just _____. Then maybe he'll just bite you."

C

IDIOMS

I. Tell whether each statement is true or false.

1. If you are <u>sitting pretty</u>, you are anxious to change jobs.

2. When your hostess <u>wouldn't hear of it</u>, you bought her a hearing aid.

3. We promised to <u>keep it to ourselves</u>, so we published it in <u>the local newspaper</u>.

4. When we saw our neighbor <u>making a pass at</u> Mr. Miller's wife, we realized <u>he liked her</u>.

II. Make up your own sentences using each of the idioms above.

D

WORD FORMS

Fill in the correct form of the words listed below.

1. ease, easy, eased, easing, easily

   a. The young man was _____ himself into the chair when she walked into the room.

   b. I can complete this exercise _____.

c. He was trying to _____ himself out of the embarrassing situation.

d. Jim thought it was _____ to swim until he tried to do it.

e. Having _____ myself into the sofa, I don't want to get up.

2. comfort, comforted, comforting

a. They tried to _____ him, but he was overcome with sorrow.

b. It is _____ to know that there is someone who cares.

c. Gloria enjoyed the _____ of her apartment.

d. The young woman _____ him by saying, "You were perfectly fine."

3. insist, insisted, insisting, insistence

a. His _____ on getting his own way made him unpopular with his friends.

b. Why did you _____ on coming to this restaurant?

c. The stranger _____ on inviting her to his party.

d. At her mother's _____, she wrote a letter to her aunt.

4. collapse, collapsed, collapsing

a. The _____ of the Roman Empire was caused by the Romans' unwillingness to fight.

b. He was so tired that he _____ in her arms.

c. The building across the street was _____ because of the earthquake.

E

PUNCTUATION

Insert commas, periods, and semicolons where necessary in the following sentences.

1. Because I was very hungry I ate four sandwiches

I ate four sandwiches because I was very hungry

I ate four sandwiches I was very hungry

2. Dinosaurs as displayed in natural history museums were very large creatures

3. Reading detective stories was Alan's favorite activity but he felt guilty about not studying

4. In 1776 the Declaration of Independence was signed

5. Professor Adams our new English teacher is a vibrant and fascinating person

6. Professor Adams is our new English teacher he is a vibrant and fascinating person

7. John had juice toast eggs and coffee for breakfast

8. In the morning I thought I had lost my wallet however I found it in my drawer later in the day

9. The book he had written became very popular even though no one understood it

10. "Look at me" he said "I bought a new suit"

F

TOPICS FOR WRITING AND DISCUSSION

1. Do people *always* forget what they did when they were drunk?

2. Describe a drunken man or woman whom you have seen.

3. In a paragraph, describe the thoughts running through Peter's mind as the woman told him about his actions of the previous evening.

Harpist on Horseback

HILDA COLE ESPY

Hilda Cole Espy is both a writer and a housewife. She lives in Mount Kisco, New York, with her family. This story about Cassie and her harp is based on Espy's true-life experiences in Mount Kisco, which are described in her book *Quiet, Yelled Mrs. Rabbit* (1958).

CASSIE WAS EIGHT the first time she mentioned that she wanted to play the harp.° Now and then she still jumped off her bed to see if she could fly like Peter Pan.° Her bedroom floor being uncarpeted, we usually knew when she had once again met with disillusionment.°

> stringed musical instrument / imaginary character in a children's story / disappointment

Her three older sisters were turning young-ladyish and making sense at that time. But Cassie was a character° who, whether she could fly or not, still managed to spend most of her time in never-never land.* Her rainy-day drawings were of frowzy° little mermaids° and frowzy little fairies° who bore a strong resemblance° to the artist. Cassie seldom combed her reddish-brown hair or tied her shoelaces or washed her neck.

> unusual or original person
>
> dirty; untidy
>
> imaginary beings with magic powers / similarity

In those days she was a genius at the irrelevant° question. I recall her asking one lovely sunny May day, "Mommy, do you think it'll rain next Halloween°?" She had many "ideers°," as she called them, and they were all so fantastic that it took heroic restraint° to deal with them patiently. While her big sisters might ask on a Saturday morning if they could walk downtown and buy some bobby pins,* Cassie would ask if she could catch the next train to New York, some fifty miles from our village of Mount Kisco, and buy a horse.

> unconnected with what is being discussed
>
> holiday in October / ideas
>
> control

One Saturday morning we were sitting around the kitchen table. Mona, Freddy, and Joanna were discussing what they'd like to be when they grew up. Mona thought she'd like to be a vet°, Freddy planned to design clothes, and Joanna decided to get married and have a lot of children. Cassie had been swiveling° her head around thoughtfully.

> animal doctor
>
> turning

mermaid

"Mommy," she chirped, "do you think I could combine riding horseback with playing the harp?"

We all fastened mirthfully° disparaging° gazes upon her. "Let's not be weird°," I teased°. "Let's have no member of this family cantering° about while playing the harp . . ." *merrily / belittling*
strange / said jokingly
galloping on a horse

Cassie glared°. Then her eyes filled with tears. *stared angrily*

"That's not what I meant!" she shouted. "I didn't mean I'd play it *on* the horse!"

And she went running upstairs to her room, letting out loud boohoos. When I followed to make up* with her, she cried, "You think everything I say is funny! I wanna° play the harp and I'm *gonna*° play the harp!" She darted° her disheveled° head at me like a small snake. *want to*
going to / moved forward
suddenly / untidy

I patted her bony little shoulder. This "ideer," like the "ideer" of buying a horse, would pass, I knew. (I thought I knew!)

In the next six months Cassie gave up attempting to fly like Peter Pan and stopped saying that she was going to marry Mel Ferrer°. But she did not stop predicting that she was going to play the harp. She managed ingeniously° to insinuate° her yen° for the instrument into all family conversations. If Mona complained of poison ivy*, Cassie would remark that she was glad *she* didn't get poison ivy, as it might interfere with her playing the harp. Let Joanna mention that she'd like ice skates for Christmas, and Cassie would smile and crowd winsomely° up against her father or me and croon°, "I know what I'd like for Christmas." *handsome actor*
cleverly / suggest, hint / desire
lovably
hum gently

That September, when the three older girls resumed piano lessons, Cassie was offered a chance to join them. She angrily refused. "You know what I want to play," she said.

I felt it was time for a showdown°. "All right, we'll go see Mr. Stochek," I said. "We'll find out how to get hold of*a harp." *an event that forces a situation to its conclusion*

Mr. Stochek sells violins, tubas, harmonicas, oboes, guitars, clarinets in Mount Kisco. He also arranges for a child to take lessons on any instrument he elects°. *chooses*

"Mr. Stochek," I said as we entered the store, "this is Cassie. She wants to take harp lessons."

"Harp lessons?" He made a why-can't-anything-go-right-today sort of face. "Why do you want to take harp lessons?"

Cassie glared at him.

"I just do," she said.

"Want to buy a harp, do you, Mrs. Espy?" he asked me dryly°. "Cost you twenty-five hundred dollars." *sarcastically; humorously*

"Of course not. Even if we had that much money, which we don't, we wouldn't want to *buy* a harp without knowing how much talent Cassie has or how hard she is willing to work."

Mr. Stochek began to shake his head.

"I don't know where you'd ever rent a harp," he said. "Even if you found one to rent, where would you find a harp teacher around here?"

I looked at Cassie. "See?" said my look. "Why don't you learn to play an instrument you could use in the school band°?" Mr. Stochek challenged Cassie. "You could march in all the parades," he suggested. "A harp's very, very hard to learn." group of persons playing music together

He reached into the glass display case* where instruments flashed and glowed. "See this here, Cassie? This is an oboe. Listen to this . . ."

He put the instrument to his lips and produced a rich oriental-sounding series of notes. Cassie stared stubbornly, refusing to be charmed.

Mr. Stochek strummed a guitar and sang a few bars of "Davy Crockett." He blew a trumpet. He played "Dark Eyes" on an accordian.

"You like that?" he'd ask Cassie after each performance.

"It's all right," she'd say, with maddening° listlessness°, "but I don't *want* to play anything until I play the harp." annoying / lack of energy or interest

Mr. Stochek sagged° against the counter°. leaned tiredly / table in a store

"Thank you," I said.

"You're welcome." His voice was very carefully controlled.

I walked Cassie out on Main Street; her eyes were spilling over with tears, and she had her mouth stuck out like a Ubangi°. member of an African tribe known for stretching the lower lip as a sign of beauty

"Now listen, Cassie," I said. "If you want to play something, you'll just have to play something that's available, that's all."

The tears rolled on.

"How can you take harp lessons if we can't get hold of a harp?" I screamed.

She marched along silently, tragically.

"Stop drizzling°!" I cried. "We tried—what more can we do?" crying; lightly raining

"I'll pray," declared Cassie. "I'll pray every night."

The following spring I made one of my rare trips to New York to lunch with a friend. Before catching the 3:20 home I decided to walk across 57th Street and window-shop° on my way to Grand Central Station. I thought this route was my own idea, but of course Cassie had been constantly in touch* with Heaven, and they're all harpists up there except for the horn player, Gabriel. Suddenly I saw a neat black sign: "Lyon and Healy. Harps." look in store windows

Cassie's face came to mind, the big gray eyes, the face drawn° with wistfulness°. As in a dream I found my way upstairs to a quiet room, gleaming° with huge golden harps. A man was sitting at a desk at the end of an aisle formed by harps. tight with worry
unsatisfied desire
shining

"I am Mark Hunzinger. What can I do for you?" he inquired cordially°.

"I have a little girl, Cassie," I began. "She gets queer° ideas. Now she wants to play the harp."

"Tell me about her," he invited. "How long has she had this idea?"

"For a couple of years," I said, twisting my gloves. "She keeps saying she wants to play one. She keeps saying she *hears* harps— in orchestrations and things."

"Well, she's beginning to sound like a real harpist!" pronounced Mr. Hunzinger. He spoke like a doctor diagnosing the mumps°.

"Most harpists, like Cassie, have had to overcome° a lot of resistance," he said. "It's not the easiest instrument to get hold of, and it's difficult to play. Did *you* ever, by any chance, want to play the harp?"

"Oh no," I said. "It never would have occurred° to me."

It seemed important to him to establish that this was Cassie's own burning idea, that she was not the daughter of a frustrated° harpist.

"She certainly should have her harp," he decided briskly. "I'll rent you one." He put his hand on a beautiful little harp, crowned like a queen. "This would be the right size for Cassie."

I gulped°.

"Don't you think perhaps we'd better think about it?" I asked. Renting the harp was expensive. Somehow I felt I hadn't communicated to Mr. Hunzinger what Cassie was really like, wanting to fly off her bed and marry Mel Ferrer.

"This is a difficult instrument and the sooner she starts the better," he said. "You can pick it up Friday, on the loading platform at Steinway Hall. And meantime, you call Lucile Lawrence, in Larchmont. She teaches the harp. I'll tell Miss Lawrence all about Cassie, and I think she'll try to arrange to teach her."

Homeward bound on a later train, it seemed to me that my life was already strewn° with abandoned° fancies of the children: unfinished knitting, puppies who were now dogs, kittens who were now cats, drum majors' batons°, and oil painting sets . . . and now it seemed I had a great big harp on my hands.

My husband and I drove the station wagon into New York on Friday night to pick up the harp. In its large wooden case it occupied the entire car except for the front seat; it required the combined muscles of my husband and Mr. Hunzinger to wedge it into place*. "She couldn't play the flute. Oh no," I said crossly°.

Cassie was waiting up for us at home. She held the door open

Glossary (right margin):

warmly, sincerely

strange, unusual

a childhood disease

get over, get beyond

come (to mind)

unfulfilled; disappointed

swallowed quickly

scattered / given up

sticks used by leaders of marching bands

irritably

gravely while we grunted° and heaved° the heavy harp case into
the living room. She did not jump up and down and clap her
hands, as she usually did when she was pleased. She stood quietly
while we lifted the harp out of the case. Then she ran one finger
up and down the strings. A strange and beautiful sound went
vibrating° through the house. She gave a sudden, radiant° smile.

made deep sounds /
lifted

echoing; shaking /
glowing

"It's just what I thought it would be like," she said.

That Sunday we drove Cassie to Larchmont for her first
lesson with Miss Lawrence—one of the many, many Sundays we
were to spend this way, an hour to Larchmont, an hour or more
for the lesson itself, an hour back.

Propped up* on a telephone book on a bench behind Miss
Lawrence's enormous concert grand harp, Cassie looked very
small. I found myself afraid for her; I didn't want her to meet
frustration.

Miss Lawrence showed her how to balance the harp and
explained how a harpist, on playing a chord°, closes his hand and
raises it, as if he had captured the sound in his palm.

three or more notes
sounded together

"Nijinsky, the dancer, worked all one summer in Maine with
Salzedo, the harpist, to develop these motions, Cassie," she said.
"An audience tends to watch a harpist. So it is important how we
look."

Cassie scuffled° and hitched° reflectively. Why, I'll bet she
starts tucking in her blouse, I thought. (She did. As she improved
on the harp, she improved in neatness.)

moved restlessly / pulled
quickly

I listened to Miss Lawrence outline the ground she expected
Cassie to cover by next week: the notes of the scales, the
functions of the seven pedals. "And, Cassie," she added, "would
you write me a piece°?"

musical composition

"All right," said Cassie, who had never read a note of music
in her life, let alone write it!

She doesn't know Cassie, I thought apprehensively°. Cassie,
the most disorganized member of the family, who had always
preferred fantastic dreams to grappling° with realities within ac-
tual reach! But Miss Lawrence did know Cassie; it was I who did
not know Cassie—the harpist.

fearfully

struggling

She learned her notes and she learned her pedals and she
composed her piece, too, and Miss Lawrence made an arrangement of it for her. It was the first thing she played after "Yankee
Doodle." (There is nothing quite like "Yankee Doodle" played
smartly on a big harp by a small girl.)

But I still had reservations° about Cassie's future on the
instrument. I wasn't a musician, but I had friends who were
musicians, and I knew how hard they had to work. I watched and

doubts

waited. And meantime learned a few things, like how to string a
harp, and how to tune° a harp.   adjust the strings of

When we planned our vacation on Cape Cod, I thought Cassie might be relieved to leave the harp behind, escape from practicing. But she wanted to take it with her.

"You see, I have more time to practice in the summer," she
said.

Miss Lawrence backed her up*, and we arranged to transport
the harp to Cape Cod.

When we returned to school that fall, Cassie had to make a
decision she'll have to make over and over and over again as time
goes on. Did she care enough about practicing the harp to forego°   do without
many of the activities in which her friends were engaging?

"I'd sorta like to go in for* cheer leading*," she said to me
wistfully, "but I can't go out for cheer leading because then I
wouldn't have enough time for my harp."

I was on the point of thinking that Cassie would never again
make my head spin with an impossible "ideer" when, one Saturday morning, I heard her ask her father to drive her to Sunnyfield
Farm. They give horseback riding lessons there.

"Now just a minute!" I whirled from the sink. "We can't afford°   have the money for
riding lessons as well as harp lessons, Cassie!"

"I know that." She nodded. "I just want to *look* at the
horses . . ."

On her return she happily reported that George, the riding
master, had let her help him groom° the horses.   clean and brush

"Some Saturdays, when the horses aren't all being ridden,
he'll let me ride after I groom them," she said. "Wasn't that nice
of George?"

My eyes narrowed. For suddenly I remembered her question,
"Do you think I could combine horseback riding with playing the
harp?"

I thought of calling George and warning him. But then I
decided, George can learn his own lessons. I'm too busy figuring
out how to buy the harp!

Most Sundays we drove Cassie to Larchmont for her lesson. It
was never dull° to listen to Miss Lawrence teaching because she   uninteresting
somehow taught much more than the harp.

"You must look at good pictures, Cassie," she told our
daughter, "and read good books. This will help you play the harp
well."

"You must use *everything*, Cassie," Miss Lawrence would
say. "You must listen with your ears as well as think with your
mind and see with your eyes that read the music."

How true! Most of us don't use everything but lean° too hard   depend
on one faculty° or another . . . our great big brains, or our great   sense; ability
big hearts . . .

In the fall of Cassie's thirteenth year, a little more than two
years after her first trip to Miss Lawrence's, she joined the
Westchester Youth Symphony in White Plains.

She got her audition° music (preludes from the opera *Car-*   trial hearing
men) in the mail two days before she was due to play for Norman
Leydon, the conductor. On Saturday morning her father and I
lifted the harp into the station wagon and drove Cassie to the
County Center Building at White Plains, for her audition.

She made the orchestra and stayed for rehearsal. And now,
every Saturday morning, we load the harp into the station wagon
at 9:15 so that Cassie can be set up and on the stage at White
Plains by 9:45. The orchestra rehearses until 12:30, and by one
o'clock we're back in Mount Kisco again.

I've said it before and I'll say it again: Cassie had better marry
a moving man. A moving man who is fond of* horses.

IDIOMS AND PHRASES*

never-never land	*imaginary residence of Peter Pan*
bobby pins	*hair pins*
make up	*become friends again after a quarrel*
poison ivy	*an itchy rash caused by the poison ivy plant*
get hold of	*get possession of*
display case	*showcase*
in touch	*talking or writing to*
wedge it into place	*fit into a tight place*
propped up	*raised*
backed her up	*supported her, agreed*
go in for	*work at*
cheer leading	*chanting and dancing in a group to encourage a team to win*
fond of	*likes, has an affection for*

A

COMPREHENSION QUESTIONS

1. How was Cassie "different"?   **2.** What were her two main interests?

3. Where did Mrs. Espy find a harp?

4. What was Cassie's reaction when she saw her harp for the first time? Was that her usual reaction to something that pleased her?

5. How did the harp improve Cassie?

6. How did the harp keep Cassie from doing other things with her friends?

7. Do you think Cassie will ever get her horse? Why?

8. How did the harp expand and improve Cassie's character?

B

VOCABULARY BUILDER

1. Write a sentence using each of the following adverbs. Be sure you know what the words mean.

Example: playfully

She ran her fingers _playfully_ through the sand.

ingeniously	mirthfully	crossly
winsomely	dryly	apprehensively

2. Now choose five adjectives from the vocabulary list below, and write a short paragraph using one of the adjectives in each sentence.

Example: Her hair was **disheveled** by the wind. Still, she ran through the **drizzling** rain. When she entered the room, her mother remarked on her **frowzy** appearance.

harp	heaved	hitched
disillusionment	vibrating	grappling
frowzy	radiant	reservations
fairies	cantering	forego
irrelevant	darted	showdown
restraint	disheveled	get hold of
swiveling	ingeniously	glared
weird	insinuate	school band
gulped	yen	maddening
strewn	poison ivy	listlessness
abandoned	croon	drizzling
grunted	scuffled	wistfulness

C

IDIOMS

Fill in the blanks by selecting the idiom from the list below that is closest in meaning to the words in parentheses.

make up with   have reservations about
stay in touch   get hold of
bears a strong resemblance   making sense
found my way

1. I wasn't _____about the confusing
        (being clear)
   incident.

2. This doll _____to the doll I had
        (looks like)
   when I was a child.

3. Let's _____with each other, even
        (keep in contact)
   though we are both leaving this school.

4. Even though I didn't speak the language clearly,

   I _____ to my aunt's house.
        (knew how to get to)

5. I don't know, I _____going
        (am doubtful about)
   into engineering as a career.

6. I will try to _____the man at the
        (reach)
   agency who handles new applications.

7. I tried very hard to _____my
        (become friends again with)
   sister after the fight.

D

WORD FORMS

Fill in the correct form of the words listed below.

1. frustrate, frustrating, frustration

   a. If she wants to study the harp, do not _____ her.

   b. She felt great _____ at not being able to ride a horse.

   c. It is _____ to study for a test and then to fail it.

2. queer, queerly, queerness

   a. Her friends thought she was _____ because she preferred studying to going to the movies.

   b. The _____ of the situation frightened her.

   c. By the anxiety in the woman's eyes, you could tell that the man with her

   was acting _____.

3. disparage, disparaging, disparagingly, disparagement

   a. He treated her _____.

   b. Don't be _____ when someone speaks English less fluently than you.

   c. Don't _____ his good intentions.

   d. The teacher's lecture to his students was full of _____.

4. apprehensive, apprehensively, apprehension

    a. Because he expected to be punished, the child looked at his mother with

    _____.

    b. Although he had done his homework, he walked to the blackboard

    _____.

    c. I am always _____ about speaking
    before a large audience.

E

"WILL" AND "WOULD"

When the verb in one clause is in the present tense, use **will** in the other clause. When the verb in one clause is in the past tense, use **would** in the other clause. Supply the correct word, **will** or **would**, in the blanks below.

Examples: If Nina complained of poison ivy, Cassie _____ remark that she was glad she didn't have it.

    If Nina complained of poison ivy, Cassie <u>would</u> remark that she was glad she didn't have it.

    It's just what I thought it _____ be like.

    It's just what I thought it <u>would</u> be like.

    I wonder if I _____ like my new teacher.

    I wonder if I <u>will</u> like my new teacher.

1. They were discussing what they _____ like to do when they finished school.

2. Please ask him when he _____ be ready to leave.

3. I _____ have the suit ready for you if you are patient.

4. _____ you tell me why you didn't call me last week?

5. "I _____ like to see you again soon," he said.

6. "_____ you please bring home a newspaper?" she asked.

7. Cassie believed that if she wanted something badly enough, it _____ happen.

8. If she continues to practice, Cassie _____ be a famous harpist someday.

9. If Cassie is serious about her music, Mrs. Espy _____ buy her a harp.

10. Cassie said she _____ like to go horseback riding in addition to playing the harp.

F

FUTURE PERFECT TENSE

The future perfect tense is used for an action that will be in the past at a given time in the future. With the future perfect we always use a time expression. Supply the future perfect tense of the verbs in parentheses.

Example: In three years' time, I will (have/had) (finish) my studies.

In three years' time, I will <u>have finished</u> my studies.

1. By the end of this month, he will (have/had) (earn) a great deal of money.

2. The snow will (have/has/had) (stop) by the time we are ready to leave.

3. By Tuesday, he will (have/had) (get) over his hangover.

4. If we don't hurry, the wedding will (have/had) (take) place before our arrival.

5. If he isn't careful, before the taxi ride is over she will (have/has/had) (convince) him to marry her.

6. Our course will (have/has/had) (start) by the end of this week.

7. Before January, they will (have/had) (take) their entrance examination for college.

8. Cassie will (have/had) (learn) to ride a horse by the end of the summer.

9. By the end of the year, you will (have/had) (perform) before a large audience.

10. When we reach India, we shall (have/had) (sail) all around the world.

G

TOPICS FOR WRITING AND DISCUSSION

1. What kind of person is Cassie's mother, Mrs. Espy?

2. Do you play a musical instrument? Which one? How has it changed your life?

3. Have you made any sacrifices in order to pursue a hobby or interest? Explain.

The Awful Fate of
Melpomenus Jones

STEPHEN LEACOCK

The following selection is another illustration of Stephen Leacock's British and Canadian background. The story presents a typically British situation — a clergyman visiting a family in their country home — in a very untypical series of events. As in the other Leacock selection, some British idioms, vocabulary, and spellings are used throughout the story. For biographical information on the author, see the introductory note to "My Financial Career," page 40.

SOME PEOPLE—not you nor I, because we are so awfully° self-possessed°—but some people, find great difficulty in saying good-bye when making a call or spending° the evening. As the moment draws near when the visitor feels that he is fairly entitled° to go away he rises and says abruptly°, "Well, I think I . . ." Then the people say, "Oh, must you go now? Surely it's early yet!" and a pitiful struggle° ensues.°

I think the saddest case of this kind of thing that I ever knew was that of my poor friend Melpomenus Jones, a curate°—such a dear° young man, and only twenty-three! He simply couldn't get away from people. He was too modest° to tell a lie, and too religious to wish to appear rude°. Now it happened that he went to call on* some friends of his on the very first afternoon of his summer vacation. The next six weeks were entirely his own—absolutely nothing to do. He chatted° awhile, drank two cups of tea, then braced° himself for the effort and said suddenly:

"Well, I think I . . ."

But the lady of the house said, "Oh, no! Mr. Jones, can't you really stay a little longer?"

Jones was always truthful. "Oh, yes," he said, "of course, I—er—can stay."

"Then please don't go."

He stayed. He drank eleven cups of tea. Night was falling. He rose again.

"Well now," he said shyly, "I think I really . . ."

"You must go?" said the lady politely. "I thought perhaps you could have stayed to dinner . . ."

"Oh well, so I could, you know," Jones said, "if . . ."

"Then please stay, I'm sure my husband will be delighted."

"All right," he said feebly°, "I'll stay," and sank back into his chair, just full of tea, and miserable.

Papa came home. They had dinner. All through the meal Jones sat planning to leave at eight-thirty. All the family wondered whether Mr. Jones was stupid and sulky°, or only stupid.

After dinner mamma undertook to "draw him out*," and

very

calm, confident

passing (a period of time)

has a right to / suddenly

fight, violent effort / follows

clergyman

warmhearted

shy, humble

impolite, not friendly

talked about unimportant things / prepared

weakly

silently angry

showed him photographs. She showed him all the family
museum, several gross° of them—photos of papa's uncle and his   °twelve dozen; a large
wife, and mamma's brother and his little boy, an awfully interest-   amount
ing photo of papa's uncle's friend in his Bengal° uniform, an   °large region in India
awfully well-taken photo of papa's grandfather's partner's dog,
and an awfully wicked one of papa as the devil for a fancy-dress
ball*.

At eight-thirty Jones had examined seventy-one photographs.
There were about sixty-nine more that he hadn't. Jones rose.

"I must say good night now," he pleaded°.   °begged

"Say good night!" they said, "why it's only half-past eight!
Have you anything to do?"

"Nothing," he admitted, and muttered° something about   °said in a low voice not
staying six weeks, and then laughed miserably.   meant to be heard

Just then it turned out that the favourite child of the family,
such a dear little romp°, had hidden Mr. Jones's hat; so papa   °playful, jumping child
said that he must stay, and invited him to a pipe and a chat. Papa
had the pipe and gave Jones the chat, and still he stayed. Every
moment he meant to take the plunge*, but couldn't. Then papa
began to get very tired of Jones, and fidgeted° and finally said, with   °moved restlessly
jocular° irony, that Jones had better stay all night, they could give   °humorous
him a shake-down°. Jones mistook his meaning and thanked him   °a bed on the floor
with tears in his eyes, and papa put Jones to bed in the spare room
and cursed him heartily°.   °sincerely

After breakfast next day, papa went off to his work in the
City, and left Jones playing with the baby, broken-hearted°. His   °suffering from deep
nerve was utterly° gone. He was meaning to leave all day, but the   sorrow / completely
thing had got on his mind and he simply couldn't. When papa
came home in the evening he was surprised and chagrined° to find   °annoyed, disappointed
Jones still there. He thought to jockey° him out with a jest, and   °direct by cleverness
said he thought he'd have to charge him for his board°, he! he! The   °meals by the week or
unhappy young man stared wildly for a moment, then wrung°   month / shook
papa's hand, paid him a month's board in advance, and broke   vigorously
down and sobbed like a child.

In the days that followed he was moody and unapproachable°.   °not friendly
He lived, of course, entirely in the drawing-room°, and the lack of   °room in which guests are
air and exercise began to tell° sadly on his health. He passed his   received / affect
time* in drinking tea and looking at the photographs. He would
stand for hours gazing° at the photographs of papa's uncle's friend   °looking long and steadily
in his Bengal uniform—talking to it, sometimes swearing bitterly
at it. His mind was visibly° failing.   °clearly

At length* the crash came. They carried him upstairs in a
raging delirium° of fever. The illness that followed was terrible.   °disorienting mental
He recognised no one, not even papa's uncle's friend in his Bengal   disturbance

uniform. At times he would start up from his bed and shriek,
"Well, I think I . . ." and then fall back upon the pillow with a
horrible laugh. Then, again, he would leap up and cry, "Another
cup of tea and more photographs! More photographs! Har! Har!"

At length, after a month of agony°, on the last day of his   great pain or suffering
vacation, he passed away*. They say that when the last moment
came, he sat up in bed with a beautiful smile of confidence
playing upon his face, and said, "Well—the angels are calling me;
I'm afraid I really must go now. Good afternoon."

And the rushing of his spirit from its prison-house was as
rapid° as a hunted cat passing over a garden fence.   quick, speedy

IDIOMS AND PHRASES*

call on	*pay a short visit to*
draw him out	*make him talk*
fancy-dress ball	*party at which fantastic or un-* *usual clothing is worn*
take the plunge	*do something decisively*
passed his time	*spent his time*
at length	*finally*
passed away	*died*

A

COMPREHENSION QUESTIONS

1. What was Jones's main problem?

2. Did Jones's piety (religiousness) contribute to his problem? How?

3. How long was his vacation supposed to last?

4. If he had not been on vacation, would Jones have found himself in the same predicament? Why?

5. How long did Jones stay with his hosts?

B

VOCABULARY BUILDER

Select the correct definition for the underlined word by circling either **a, b, c,** or **d.**

1. The patient made a <u>rapid</u> recovery.

a. fearful
b. joyful

c. speedy
d. unusual

2. The host greeted them <u>heartily</u> and offered them a drink.

   a. cautiously   **c.** sincerely
   b. coldly   **d.** gently

3. The baby <u>fidgeted</u> in his highchair, longing to go out and play.

   a. cried   **c.** moved restlessly
   b. played   **d.** ate

4. The clerk <u>muttered</u> under his breath as he brought the customer the tenth pair of shoes.

   a. whistled   **c.** chuckled
   b. spoke in a low voice   **d.** cried

5. She was <u>awfully</u> upset about his leaving.

   a. very   **c.** weakly
   b. slightly   **d.** clearly

6. She <u>chatted</u> on for a while, not realizing that her listener had fallen asleep.

   a. chewed   **c.** cried
   b. spoke   **d.** sang

7. "No matter what <u>ensues</u>," the heroine said to herself, "I will tell the truth."

   a. falls down   **c.** begins
   b. joins in   **d.** results

8. He was <u>chagrined</u> to find that he had forgotten his guest's name.

   a. annoyed   **c.** unprepared
   b. confused   **d.** delighted

9. "Please," she <u>pleaded</u>, "don't let the reporters see me with my hair uncombed."

   a. called   **c.** begged
   b. yelled   **d.** promised

10. When I <u>called on</u> him, his wife said he was out.

   a. telephoned   **c.** wrote
   b. chose   **d.** visited

11. An employee is <u>entitled to</u> a lunch period.

   a. has a right to   **c.** cannot have
   b. wants   **d.** needs

12. The patient lifted her head <u>feebly</u> from the pillow.

a. eagerly   **c.** in pain
b. weakly   **d.** longingly

13. The <u>struggle</u> for survival is fierce among jungle animals.

a. fight   **c.** advantage
b. plan   **d.** dream

14. "You're too <u>modest</u>," the critic said. "I enjoyed seeing you act."

a. tall   **c.** humble
b. loud   **d.** proud

15. I was <u>utterly</u> enchanted by your singing.

a. completely   **c.** amazingly
b. quietly   **d.** recklessly

16. When she doesn't get her way, she becomes <u>sulky</u>.

a. distressed   **c.** gay
b. reckless   **d.** silently angry

C

IDIOMS

1. Expressions with **mean.**

   a. mean = to have in mind

      I <u>mean</u> to go to England someday.

   b. mean business = to really mean it, be serious

      The teacher said she would fail the students who didn't study, and she <u>meant business</u>.

   c. by all means = certainly, without fail

      She felt that she should <u>by all means</u> help Harry find a job.

   d. by means of = by the use of, with the help of

      <u>By means of</u> an education, people can now obtain better jobs.

Write four sentences of your own using each of these definitions of **mean.**

2. Expressions with **draw.**

a. draw up = to put in writing, compose

The two countries <u>drew up</u> an agreement for a cease-fire.

b. draw out = to take out, remove

He <u>drew</u> the cork <u>out</u> of the bottle.

c. draw a long breath = to breathe deeply when getting ready to speak or act

The teacher <u>drew a long breath</u> when she saw her most uncooperative student approach.

d. draw the line = to refuse to go as far as

Although they were tired, they <u>drew the line</u> at taking a taxi.

e. draw back = to move back, step backward

The children <u>drew back</u> from the cat when it scratched them.

Write five sentences of your own using each of these definitions of **draw.**

D

FORMS OF OBLIGATION

Ought to, should, and **must** have approximately the same meaning, and all are used to suggest obligation. **Must,** however, cannot be used for the past tense. Supply **should, ought to,** or **must** in the following sentences, along with the correct form of the verb in parentheses. Follow the examples.

Examples: You _____ (finish) your reading.

You <u>ought to finish</u> your reading.

I (know) I _____ .

I <u>know</u> I <u>should.</u>

You _____ (not) (smoke); smoking causes cancer.

You <u>must not smoke</u>; smoking causes cancer.

I _____ (study) for the exam last week.

I <u>should have studied</u> for the exam last week.

1. In order to keep them shiny, you ⎯⎯⎯⎯⎯ (polish) your shoes every night.

2. You ⎯⎯⎯⎯⎯⎯⎯⎯⎯⎯⎯⎯ (not) (spend) more money than you earn.

3. I ⎯⎯⎯⎯⎯⎯⎯⎯⎯⎯⎯ (warn) him about the test yesterday.

4. You ⎯⎯⎯⎯⎯⎯⎯⎯⎯ (wait) for me on Forty-second Street where we agreed to meet.

5. I ⎯⎯⎯⎯⎯⎯⎯⎯⎯⎯ (answer) his letter yesterday.

6. I ⎯⎯⎯⎯⎯⎯⎯⎯⎯⎯⎯ (study) every night.

7. They ⎯⎯⎯⎯⎯⎯⎯⎯ (not) (waste) so much time at work.

8. In order to stay healthy, he ⎯⎯⎯⎯⎯⎯⎯⎯⎯⎯ (have) a yearly checkup.

9. "I ⎯⎯⎯⎯⎯⎯⎯⎯ (leave) now," said Melpomenus Jones.

10. When ⎯⎯⎯⎯⎯⎯⎯⎯ you (take) your driver's test?

11. ⎯⎯⎯⎯⎯⎯⎯ you (go) now or can you wait a little longer?

12. Last week, ⎯⎯⎯⎯⎯⎯⎯ you (pay) customs duty on the carpet that arrived at the port?

13. "You ⎯⎯⎯⎯⎯⎯⎯⎯⎯ (not) (play) with matches," said the mother to her four-year-old child.

14. If Joan comes in after midnight, she ⎯⎯⎯⎯⎯⎯⎯⎯⎯⎯. (come) in quietly; she woke me up last night.

15. You ⎯⎯⎯⎯⎯⎯⎯ (make) your bed when you join the army.

16. If there will be no taxis, we ⎯⎯⎯⎯⎯⎯⎯⎯ (walk).

17. If we want to hear all the arias, we ⎯⎯⎯⎯⎯⎯⎯⎯⎯ (not) (be) late for the opera.

18. You ⎯⎯⎯⎯⎯⎯⎯⎯⎯ (not) (speak) like that to your father.

E

PAST CONTINUOUS TENSE

The past continuous tense describes a past action that is continuing at the time of another past action. Note that the first verb phrase (past continuous) takes the -ing form, while the second verb phrase takes the simple past tense.

I. Supply the past continuous form (-ing) of the verbs in parentheses.

Examples: He _____ to leave all day, but the thing had got on
(mean)
his mind, and he simply couldn't.

He <u>was meaning</u> to leave all day, but the thing had got on his mind, and he simply couldn't.

He _____ in the mirror when she walked in.
(look)
He <u>was looking</u> in the mirror when she walked in.

1. Jones _____ himself to leave when the lady of the house
(brace)
served tea.

2. Mary _____ when I went to see her last night.
(read)

3. Melpomenus Jones _____ at photographs when Papa
(look)
arrived.

4. We _____ at Kennedy Airport when the accident
(land)
occurred.

5. When I arrived home, the sun _____.
(set)

6. He _____ with the children when the doorbell rang.
(chat)

7. The children _____ when we walked into the classroom.
(play)

8. While we _____, Mary telephoned.
(wait)

9. As I _____ into the house, I tripped on a toy.
(walk)

10. She fell while she _____ out of the car.
(get)

II. Fill in the blanks with verbs in the past continuous tense. Choose your own verbs.

1. My sister ————————————— while I washed the dishes.

2. As I walked into the class, the teacher ————————————.

3. When I arrived home, my parents ————————————.

4. My employer ————————————— when I walked into the office.

5. I ————————————— when I received your letter.

III. Change each of the following sentences from simple past time to continuous past time, and add a clause by using **when** and the simple past tense.

Example: He ate dinner.

   He <u>was eating</u> dinner when I telephoned him.

1. She drank tea last night.

2. He stayed home.

3. He played with the children.

4. They looked at photographs.

5. I paid my rent.

6. He spent his vacation at home.

7. They walked to the beach.

8. We wrote a letter to the president of the United States.

9. She left the house.

10. They went shopping.

F

TOPICS FOR WRITING AND DISCUSSION

1. Have you ever had visitors who overstayed? How did you get them to leave?

2. Do you think people who stay too long really want to stay on?

3. What other situations can you think of in which people are polite and don't really mean what they say?

4. Describe a situation in which being polite might get you into the same kind of trouble as it got Melpomenus Jones.

The Soft Sell*

ART BUCHWALD

This second selection by Art Buchwald makes fun of a student who thinks she is an expert on human behavior because she has studied psychology. The story tells how she tries to use her newfound knowledge on the customers who come into a store. The story is from *I Never Danced at the White House*. For biographical information on Art Buchwald, see the introductory note to "The Time Killer," page 14.

ONE OF THE PROBLEMS with today's economy is that it's very hard to find young people who are good salesmen. Many students coming out of college are more interested in a customer's motivation° than they are in closing° a sale. They also have a tendency to be too honest, which can play havoc* in the retail business*.

reason for doing
something / completing

A friend of mine has a dress shop here in Georgetown, and she told me of the problems she had with a young lady, a psychology major*, whom she hired as a salesgirl.

This, in essence*, is what happened:

The first day a lady came in the store, and the salesgirl (let us call her Miss Brampton) asked if she could be of help.

"I'd like a suit for the fall," the lady said.

"What price range*?" Miss Brampton asked.

"It doesn't make any difference*," the lady replied.

"Well, let me ask you this question: Do you want the suit because you need it? Or have you just had a fight with your husband and are trying to get even* by making a very expensive purchase°?"

something bought

"I beg your pardon?" the lady said.

"Perhaps you suspect° him of some infidelity°, and you think this is the only way you can get back* at him."

have an idea or
feeling / disloyalty or
unfaithfulness

"I have no idea what you're talking about," the customer said.

"Spending money in anger is a very expensive form of hostility°. My advice to you is to think it over for a few days. Try to patch up* your differences. Buying a new suit won't save your marriage."

undirected anger

"Thank you very much," the customer said frostily° and left the store.

coldly; in an unfriendly
way

"She's angry with me now," Miss Brampton told the dress shop owner, "but in a week she'll be grateful I talked her out of it*."

My friend the shop proprietor° decided to let the incident° pass; but that afternoon another customer came in, and Miss Brampton asked if she could be of help.

owner / happening

The lady said, "I need something really exciting. I'm going to the Kennedy Center, and I want a dress that will knock everyone dead*."

Miss Brampton said, "We have some lovely evening dresses over here for insecure° people."   *unsure, without self-confidence*

"Insecure people?"

"Oh, yes. Didn't you know that clothes are one of the main ways women compensate° for insecurity?"   *make up*

"I'm not insecure," the lady said angrily.

"Then why do you want to knock them dead at the Kennedy Center? Why can't you be accepted for yourself instead of what you wear? You are a very attractive person, and you have an inner beauty you try to disguise°. I can sell you a new dress that will   *hide*
attract attention*, but then you would never know if it were you or the dress that made people stop and stare°."   *look fixedly*

By this time the dress shop owner decided to step in.

"Miss Brampton, if the lady wants an evening dress, let her see our evening dresses."

"No," the customer said. "Your girl is right. Why spend five hundred dollars to get a few compliments from people who really don't care what I wear? Thank you for helping me, young lady. It's true I've been insecure all these years and didn't even know it."

The customer walked out of the store.

The final straw* for the dress store owner took place an hour later when a coed° came in to buy a hotpants° outfit, and Miss   *female student at a coeducational university / very short shorts / thirty-minute speech / liberation*
Brampton gave her thirty minutes° on women's lib° and then said, "All you do when you buy hotpants is become a sex object."

That night the dress shop owner put a sign in the window:
HELP WANTED—NO PSYCHOLOGY MAJORS NEED APPLY.

IDIOMS AND PHRASES*

soft sell	*a manner of selling without pressuring the customer*
play havoc	*cause ruin and chaos*
retail business	*stores that sell goods to the public*
psychology major	*student who specializes in the study of psychology in college*
in essence	*basically*
what price range?	*how much money do you want to spend?*
it doesn't make any difference	*it's not important, it doesn't matter*

get even	*get revenge*
get back at him	*hurt (him) back*
patch up	*put together in a hurried way;*
	repair the damage
talked her out of it	*persuaded her to change her mind*
knock everyone dead	*impressed everyone*
attract attention	*get the attention of others*
final straw	*the event or happening that made*
	it intolerable

A

COMPREHENSION QUESTIONS

Is the statement true or false? (If it's false, explain *why*.)

1. It's easy to find good salespeople.

2. Honesty is the best policy in the retail business.

3. Miss Brampton told the coed not to buy hotpants.

4. Miss Brampton made the woman who came in to buy an evening gown very happy.

5. The woman who wanted a suit suspected her husband of infidelity, and she appreciated the salesgirl's advice.

6. The store proprietor fired the salesgirl.

7. The proprietor would hire only psychology majors from now on.

8. A person's motivation is very important to psychologists.

9. You should wear an evening dress to go to the Kennedy Center.

10. "All you do when you buy hotpants is become a sex object."

B

VOCABULARY BUILDER

Answer the questions briefly, either orally or in writing.

1. Is it polite to <u>stare</u>? Why?

2. Are <u>insecure</u> people more nervous than others?

3. Is <u>infidelity</u> a major cause of divorce?

4. Do you ever try to <u>disguise</u> your <u>hostility</u>?

5. Do you <u>suspect</u> the author is not really serious?

6. What's the best way to <u>patch up</u> differences?

7. When someone looks at you <u>frostily</u>, are you upset?

8. How did the <u>proprietor</u> of the dress shop handle the <u>hotpants</u> incident?

C

IDIOMS

1. Answer the questions in complete sentences.

    a. How does psychology <u>play havoc</u> with retail business?

    b. When you try to <u>get back</u> at someone, do you sometimes hurt yourself?

    c. What do you wear when you try to <u>knock everyone dead</u>?

    d. Did the salesgirl try to <u>patch up</u> her differences with the proprietor?

    e. What was the <u>final straw</u> in the relationship between Miss Brampton and the proprietor?

2. Make up five sentences of your own, using each of the underlined idioms in the sentences above.

D

CLOTHING

1. Suppose you were going on (a) a business trip to Alaska and (b) a vacation trip to Florida. Make a list of the clothing you would need in each place and the fabrics best suited for each climate.

2. If you had to have your clothes altered, would you know what instructions to give the tailor or dressmaker? On the next page are some sketches of a dress, a pair of slacks, and a jacket. Pretend that they are (a) too large and (b) too small for you, and write instructions for

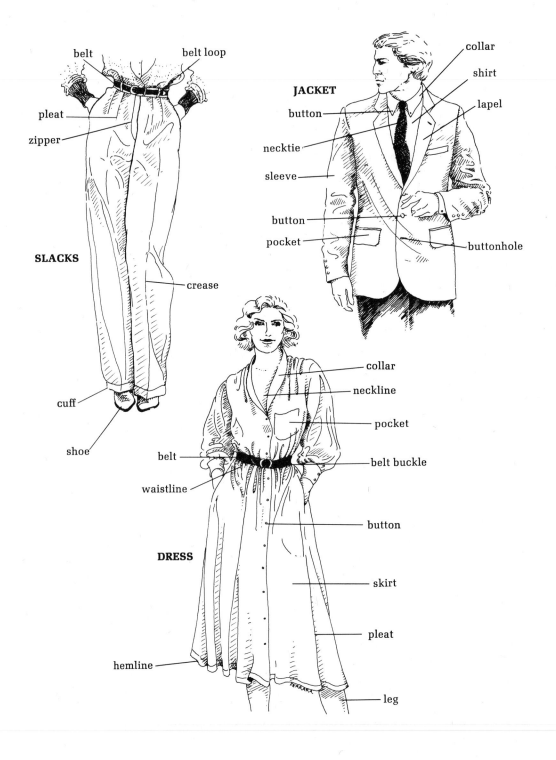

belt · belt loop

JACKET

collar · shirt · lapel

button · necktie · sleeve

button · pocket · buttonhole

pleat · zipper

SLACKS

crease

cuff · shoe

collar · neckline · pocket

belt · waistline · belt buckle

button

DRESS

skirt

pleat

hemline · leg

the necessary alterations. Be specific about what you want done, and give specific measurements.

Example: Take in the waist by three-quarters of an inch, loosen the bodice by one inch, etc.

E

INFINITIVES AND GERUNDS

Fill in the correct form—the infinitive or the gerund—of the verbs in parentheses.

Examples: My advice to you is _____ it over for a few days.
(think)
My advice to you is <u>to think</u> it over for a few days.

Try _____ up your differences.
(patch)
Try <u>to patch</u> up your differences.

Jane avoided _____ it over.
(think)
Jane avoided <u>thinking it</u> over.

John enjoys _____ up a quarrel with his wife.
(patch)
John enjoys <u>patching</u> up a quarrel with his wife.

1. These days, it is very unusual _____ young people who
   (find)
   are good salespersons.

2. Have you ever considered _____ a hotpants outfit?
   (buy)

3. I couldn't resist _____ that dress.
   (try on)

4. Why do you want _____ them dead?
   (knock)

5. The salesgirl promised _____ customers.
   (encourage)

6. I expect _____ a lovely gown soon.
   (purchase)

7. For a while, the coed considered _____ her studies.
   (give up)

8. Keep on _____. I don't want _____
   (sell)   (lose)
   money.

9. Arthur delayed ——————————— the store as long as possible.
(close)

10. The dress shop failed ——————————— the customer that her
(notify)
dresses were ready.

11. The dress shop proprietor admitted ——————————— very little
(know)
about women's lib.

12. Jane resisted ——————————— the changing fashions in women's
(understand)
clothes.

13. Fred avoids ——————————— his bills as long as possible.
(pay)

14. Miss Brampton claims ——————————— an expert on human
(be)
behavior.

15. The final straw took place when she decided ——————————— the
(discourage)
sale of an evening gown.

16. I need ——————————— a new suit.
(get)

17. I don't want ——————————— ——————————— the
(risk)   (insult)
customers.

18. Why don't you offer ——————————— him choose a new shirt?
(help)

19. Why did you refuse ——————————— her the dress?
(sell)

20. "Have you considered ——————————— another job?" the
(take)
proprietor asked.

F

"ADVISE" AND "ADVICE"

Advise (or **advised**) is a verb, while **advice** is a noun. Supply the correct word in the
following sentences. Follow each sentence with a similar example of your own.

Examples: My _____ to you is to think it over for a few days.

My <u>advice</u> to you is to think it over for a few days.

The doctor _____ complete rest after the operation.

The doctor <u>advised</u> complete rest after the operation.

1. I would _____ you to sell the stock.

2. That was sound _____.

3. When I want your _____, I'll ask for it.

4. In foreign policy, it is the Senate's responsibility to _____ and consent.

5. Giving _____ is easy; following it is difficult.

6. Don't give _____ where it's not wanted.

7. The saleswoman _____ her to buy the blue dress because it suited her.

8. My _____ is to take your English courses early in your college career.

9. A nutritionist can _____ you about preparing meals for your school.

10. Her _____ should be taken seriously.

G

TOPICS FOR WRITING AND DISCUSSION

1. Before you make a purchase in a store, do you think it over carefully, or do you buy on impulse? What was your last clothing purchase, and why did you decide to buy that particular item?

2. If you were the owner of a dress shop, would you hire psychology majors? Can you name any instances where psychology might help you to close a sale?

3. Suppose it is a store that sells men's clothing. What would you stress in order to sell a suit? A sweater? A shirt? Why?

4. Teen-agers often buy their own clothes. If you were trying to sell to a teen-ager (someone between fifteen and eighteen years old), what kinds of things would you stress?

5. When choosing a place to buy clothes, what do you look for—low prices, interested salespeople, latest styles, or what?

6. Role-playing: with a friend, act out the roles of salesperson and shopper. Pretend you have come into the store to buy a pair of shoes. Be sure to talk about color, size, price range, style, and the occasion for which you are buying them.

Glove Purchase in Gibraltar

SAMUEL CLEMENS
(MARK TWAIN)

Samuel Clemens (1835–1910) was born in Missouri, grew up on the Mississippi River, and left school at the age of twelve when his father died. He then held a variety of odd jobs, mainly as a printer and as apprentice to the pilot of a steamboat on the Mississippi, the greatest river in the United States. His familiar pen name of Mark Twain was a common slang phrase of the river pilots. He is considered the best—and the most widely read—American writer of humor and satire. His books include the travel books *Roughing It* (1872) and *Life on the Mississippi* (1883) and the world-renowned classics, *The Adventures of Tom Sawyer* (1876) and *Huckleberry Finn* (1884), which are regarded by critics as his finest works.

In June of 1867, Twain joined a party traveling on the ship *Quaker City* to the Mediterranean and Palestine. This proved to be a crucial point in his career. The book that grew out of his journey, *The Innocents Abroad* (1869), established his literary reputation. After a stop in the Azores, the ship visited Gibraltar, and the following selection describes one of Twain's experiences there.

EVERY NOW AND THEN my glove purchase in Gibraltar last night intrudes° itself upon me. Dan and the ship's surgeon and I had been up to the great square, listening to the music of the fine military bands, and contemplating° English and Spanish female loveliness and fashion, and, at 9 o'clock, were on our way to the theatre, when we met the General, the Judge, the Commodore, the Colonel, and the Commissioner of the United States of America to Europe, Asia, and Africa, who had been to the Club House, to register their several titles and impoverish° the bill of fare*, and they told us to go over to the little variety store, near the Hall of Justice, and buy some kid° gloves. They said they were elegant, and very moderate in price. It seemed a stylish thing to go to the theatre in kid gloves, and we acted upon the hint. A very handsome young lady in the store offered me a pair of blue gloves. I did not want blue, but she said they would look very pretty on a hand like mine. The remark touched° me tenderly. I glanced furtively° at my hand, and somehow it did seem rather a comely° member°. I tried a glove on my left, and blushed a little. Manifestly° the size was too small for me. But I felt gratified° when she said:

"Oh, it is just right!"—yet I knew it was no such thing.

I tugged° at it diligently, but it was discouraging work. She said:

"Ah! I see *you* are accustomed to wearing kid gloves—but some gentlemen are *so* awkward° about putting them on."

It was the last compliment I had expected. I only understand putting on the buckskin° article perfectly. I made another effort,

forces

looking at; thinking about

cause to become poor or less

leather from a young goat's skin

affected
secretly
nice-looking (old use) / part of the body / obviously / pleased

pulled

clumsy

a type of leather

128

and tore the glove from the base of the thumb into the palm of the hand—and tried to hide the rent°. She kept up her compliments, and I kept up my determination to deserve them or die:

"Ah, you have had experience!" [A rip down the back of the hand.] "They are just right for you—your hand is very small—if they tear you need not pay for them." [A rent across the middle.] "I can always tell when a gentleman understands putting on kid gloves. There is a grace about it that only comes with long practice." [The whole afterguard of the glove "fetched away°," as the sailors say, the fabric parted° across the knuckles°, and nothing was left but a melancholy° ruin°.

I was too much flattered° to make an exposure, and throw the merchandise on the angel's hands. I was hot, vexed°, confused, but still happy; but I hated the other boys for taking such an absorbing° interest in the proceedings° I wished they were in Jericho. I felt exquisitely mean° when I said cheerfully,—

"This one does very well; it fits elegantly. I like a glove that fits. No, never mind*, ma'am, never mind; I'll put the other on in the street. It is warm here."

It *was* warm. It was the warmest place I ever was in. I paid the bill, and as I passed out with a fascinating bow, I thought I detected a light in the woman's eye that was gently ironical; and when I looked back from the street, and she was laughing all to herself about something or other, I said to myself, with withering° sarcasm, "Oh, certainly; *you* know how to put on kid gloves, don't you?—a self-complacent° ass°, ready to be flattered out of your senses by every petticoat° that chooses to take the trouble to do it!"

The silence of the boys annoyed me. Finally, Dan said, musingly:

"Some gentlemen don't know how to put on kid gloves at all; but some do."

tear

came apart
separated
sad/damaged remains
pleased
annoyed

completely taking up the
attention or thoughts /
actions / ungenerous

causing somebody to
feel ashamed or
confused / satisfied with
oneself / idiot; donkey /
woman's underskirt (slang:
woman)

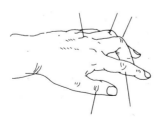

knuckles

And the doctor said (to the moon, I thought,)

"But it is always easy to tell when a gentleman is used to putting on kid gloves."

Dan soliloquized°, after a pause: talked to himself

"Ah, yes; there is a grace about it that only comes with long, very long practice."

"Yes, indeed, I've noticed that when a man hauls° on a kid   pulls with effort
glove like he was dragging° a cat out of an ash-hole by the tail, *he*   pulling
understands putting on kid gloves; *he's* had ex—"

"Boys, enough of a thing's enough! You think you are very smart, I suppose, but I don't. And if you go and tell any of those old gossips in the ship about this thing, I'll never forgive you for it; that's all."

They let me alone* then, for the time being. We always let each other alone in time to prevent ill° feeling from spoiling a   bad; sick
joke. But they had bought gloves, too, as I did. We threw all the purchases away together this morning. They were coarse°, unsub-   of poor quality, rough
stantial, freckled° all over with broad yellow splotches°, and could   dotted / spots
neither stand wear nor public exhibition. We had entertained an angel unawares, but we did not take her in*. She did that for us.

IDIOMS AND PHRASES *

bill of fare	*menu*
never mind	*don't trouble about it*
let me alone	*stayed away from me*
did not take her in	*did not fool her*

A

COMPREHENSION QUESTIONS

1. Who suggested that they buy gloves?

2. Did the author really seem used to wearing kid gloves? Why does the salesgirl flatter him so?

3. When the author looked back, was the salesgirl laughing at him or "all to herself about something or other"?

4. Compare this salesgirl with the one in "The Soft Sell." Which was more successful?

5. Why did it suddenly get so warm in the store?

6. Why did his companions laugh at our hero? Did they get taken in, also?

7. Why didn't the author refuse to buy the gloves?

B

VOCABULARY BUILDER

Select the correct definition of the underlined word by circling, **a, b, c,** or **d.**

1. When you ask to see the bill of fare, you are asking for the
   - **a.** register
   - **b.** menu
   - **c.** timetable
   - **d.** shopping list

2. A coarse fabric is
   - **a.** soft
   - **b.** printed
   - **c.** rough
   - **d.** silly

3. When you watch the proceedings, you watch
   - **a.** mirror
   - **b.** television
   - **c.** children
   - **d.** actions

4. An awkward motion is
   - **a.** clumsy
   - **b.** graceful
   - **c.** funny
   - **d.** magnificent

5. A comely child is
   - **a.** coming in
   - **b.** handsome
   - **c.** leaving
   - **d.** ugly

6. An impoverished uncle is
   - **a.** poor
   - **b.** rich
   - **c.** old
   - **d.** dead

7. A red petticoat is a (n)
   - **a.** scarf
   - **b.** shirt
   - **c.** underskirt
   - **d.** evening gown

8. When the actor is gratified by the reviews, he is
   - **a.** pleased
   - **b.** upset
   - **c.** surprised
   - **d.** irritated

9. An <u>absorbing</u> book is

    a. long   **c.** interesting
    b. dull   **d.** old

10. <u>Contemplating</u> a story is

    a. describing it   **c.** thinking about it
    b. writing it   **d.** burying it

11. A man who <u>intrudes</u> upon another's privacy

    a. forces himself   **c.** steals his silver
    b. discusses   **d.** makes a joke

12. When an actor <u>soliloquizes</u>, he speaks

    a. to himself   **c.** in a whisper
    b. to another actor   **d.** in a chorus

13. The small boy who <u>tugged</u> at his father's sleeve

    a. pulled it   **c.** pushed it
    b. threw mud at it   **d.** bit it

14. She was <u>touched</u> by the story because it was

    a. funny   **c.** long
    b. sad   **d.** short

15. No one saw the spy because he moved <u>furtively</u>. He moved

    a. secretly   **c.** noisily
    b. slowly   **d.** gracefully

16. <u>Kid</u> gloves are made of

    a. suede   **c.** cotton
    b. goatskin   **d.** wool

17. In Italy you can visit many <u>ruins</u>. Ruins are buildings that have been

    a. freshly painted   **c.** newly designed
    b. rebuilt   **d.** badly damaged

18. A teacher who is <u>vexed</u> by his students is

    a. annoyed   **c.** pleased
    b. complimented   **d.** respected

19. Something that is <u>manifestly untrue</u> is

    a. obviously a lie
    b. partially a lie

    c. completely true
    d. greatly exaggerated

20. In the old days, teachers rapped your <u>knuckles</u> when you were bad. They hit your

    a. feet
    b. hands

    c. shoulders
    d. face

C

IDIOMS WITH "HAND"

1. hand down = to arrange to give or leave after death, or after outgrowing

Mary will have her mother's pearls because they are **handed down** in the family.

2. hand in glove = very close or friendly; working together; in very close agreement or cooperation, especially for bad purposes

The detectives and the police sometimes work **hand in glove** to catch a criminal.

3. hand in hand = holding hands

Janet and Alex walked **hand in hand** down the street.

4. hand it to = to admit the excellence of, give credit or praise to

You have to **hand it to** Mark; he always gets what he wants.

5. out of hand = out of control

The teacher was so inexperienced that the class soon got **out of hand.**

6. handle with kid gloves = to treat very gently and carefully

Sandy is so sensitive that she has to be **handled with kid gloves.**

7. hand-pick = to choose very carefully

Because the job was difficult, the senator **hand-picked** his assistant.

8. hands down = easily

Because of the excellence of their players, the Yankees won the game **hands down.**

9. a free hand = great freedom

The principal gave the teacher **a free hand** in choosing her materials.

10. lend a hand = to help

When the new family moved onto the block, all the neighbors **lent a hand.**

Write ten sentences of your own using each of these expressions with **hand.**

D

WORD FORMS

Fill in the correct form of the words listed below.

1. intrude, intruded, intruding, intrusion, intruder

   a. Your opening my mail is an unnecessary _____ on my privacy.

   b. "I hope I'm not _____," he said as he walked into the room.

   c. Yesterday, the sound of the radio _____ on my concentration.

   d. The _____ set off the burglar alarm when he climbed in through the window.

   e. "Don't _____ in their lives," she advised her mother.

2. flatter, flattering, flatterer, flattered, flattery

   a. "_____ will get you nowhere," she said sweetly.

   b. Candlelight is very _____ to the skin.

   c. The teacher felt very _____ when the student told her he enjoyed her lesson.

   d. A _____ is not always sincere.

   e. If you _____ him enough, he will buy the kid gloves even though they don't fit.

3. absorb, absorbing, absorption, absorbed

    a. Can the students _____ such a difficult lesson at one time?

    b. They read the book with complete _____.

    c. Proofreading a manuscript is an _____ task.

    d. He was so _____ in the novel that he didn't hear Mother calling him to dinner.

4. contemplate, contemplated, contemplation, contemplating

    a. Are you _____ a trip to Europe this summer?

    b. Give me a chance to _____, and I might come up with an idea for the party.

    c. We _____ buying the house on Maple Street but decided against it.

    d. The _____ of children playing in the park can be quite educational.

E

CONDITIONAL: POSSIBLE

The conditional statement is composed of two clauses, the **if** clause and the **result** clause. One type of conditional statement is used when it is possible for the condition to be fulfilled. It is expressed by using the present tense in the **if** clause and the future tense in the **result** clause.

Example: If I study, I _____ pass the test.

    If I study, I <u>will</u> pass the test.

I. Write a result clause for each of the following conditional statements. Choose your own verbs.

    1. If I walk to school, I _____.

    2. If you make too much noise, you _____.

3. If they fly to Florida, they ⎯⎯⎯⎯⎯⎯⎯⎯⎯⎯⎯⎯⎯⎯⎯⎯.

4. If I learn to drive, I ⎯⎯⎯⎯⎯⎯⎯⎯⎯⎯⎯⎯⎯⎯⎯⎯⎯.

5. If we buy the house, we ⎯⎯⎯⎯⎯⎯⎯⎯⎯⎯⎯⎯⎯⎯⎯⎯.

6. If we sell the car, we ⎯⎯⎯⎯⎯⎯⎯⎯⎯⎯⎯⎯⎯⎯⎯⎯.

7. If he goes on vacation, he ⎯⎯⎯⎯⎯⎯⎯⎯⎯⎯⎯⎯⎯⎯⎯.

8. If I get lost, I ⎯⎯⎯⎯⎯⎯⎯⎯⎯⎯⎯⎯⎯⎯⎯⎯⎯⎯.

9. If she plants tomatoes, she ⎯⎯⎯⎯⎯⎯⎯⎯⎯⎯⎯⎯⎯⎯.

10. If it rains, it ⎯⎯⎯⎯⎯⎯⎯⎯⎯⎯⎯⎯⎯⎯⎯⎯⎯⎯.

II. Make up ten of your own sentences using the above form.

F

TOPICS FOR WRITING AND DISCUSSION

1. Describe how you were once talked into a purchase by a salesperson.

2. What are some other ways in which a tourist can be "taken in" in a foreign country? Has this ever happened to you?

3. Certain countries are noted for certain products, and shopping for those products is part of the pleasure of being in that country. What would you shop for in

   a. France   **c.** Italy
   b. England   **d.** China

4. In your own words, write a summary of the first paragraph of the story.

What Do You Do with Your Old Coffee Grounds?*

HOWARD LINDSAY

Howard Lindsay (1889–1968) was a noted playwright, director, and actor. In 1934 he began a collaboration with Russel Crouse that was to last twenty-eight years. Together they wrote the play *State of the Union*, which won a Pulitzer Prize in 1946. They also wrote the movie version of *The Sound of Music* in 1959, which became one of the most financially successful motion pictures ever made. Lindsay is best known for his play *Life with Father* — based on the novel by Clarence Day — which set a Broadway record of 3,224 performances over seven years. Lindsay played the father opposite his wife, Dorothy Stickney, as the mother. She is the bride he describes in the following story. They were married in 1927.

W E HAD BEEN MARRIED FOR SIX MONTHS before my wife and my mother met. The first confrontation° had its surprises as well as its difficulties. The first surprise came to my mother. She knew I had married an actress. I am sure she had imagined her to be somewhat° like the lush° female on the poster of "The Girl from Rector's." She was not prepared for that wide-eyed chit of a child* stretched out on the couch, her pale forehead contracted° in pain. I explained to mother that Dorothy was not well. She had a severe° headache. All her life mother had been subject to* what were then called "sick headaches" and she was instantly sympathetic. What we could not tell mother was that Dorothy was suffering from her first hangover°.

The night before, Dorothy and I had been down in the Village at a party. It was given by one of the gayest and most charming couples in New York, Miriam Hopkins and Bill Parker. We drank more than our wont°. At that time Dorothy hadn't cultivated° any wont and knew nothing of the consequences° of drinking too much. We had talked and laughed and sung and at six in the morning Miriam cooked us some breakfast. There just aren't any parties like that any more, unless they are being given by people who are as young now as we were then. That Dorothy was to meet her mother-in-law the next day seemed unimportant.

Mother was a small, delicate-looking woman, a wisp° of New England granite°. We had a part-time maid, which I knew struck mother as* an extravagance°, but she held her peace*. I had ordered a simple and frugal° dinner which mother seemed to enjoy. Dorothy sat with us at the table, ate little, and contributed less to the conversation. After the coffee had been served, mother held Dorothy's eye* and asked, "What do you do with your old coffee grounds?" The throb° in Dorothy's temple° jumped into high gear*. Had my wife been in perfect health and high spirits*, I submit° this was an unfair question. "I don't know what we do

meeting

in a way / luxuriant

compressed; wrinkled
serious; painful

unpleasant physical effects following the heavy use of alcohol

custom, habit / developed
effects, results

small piece
very hard stone
too much; an extreme
economical, inexpensive

pulse / side of the forehead

state

138

with them," she stammered°, looking very guilty. "I guess we just   spoke haltingly
throw them away." "You can use them for flavoring," mother
said smugly°. "Make your own coffee jello."   in a self-satisfied way

I, too, had been bewildered° by mother's question, but now I   puzzled
knew that mother had accepted our marriage and was trying to
contribute to it. And all she had to contribute were the economies
that a lifetime of being poor had taught her. She knew all the
shortcuts and shifts° that would save a penny, and to her not   tricks
saving a penny when you could was one of the deadly sins. A
worse sin, if there was one, was spending a penny you didn't need
to spend.

Ten years before my marriage I had been able to bring mother
to New York for a visit. I thought she deserved a fling° and in my   celebration
ignorance thought she would enjoy one. The first night I took her
to dinner at Mouquin's. In those days you could get a good Italian
dinner anywhere for seventy-five cents and if you knew your New
York you could get a substantial° meal for forty or fifty cents.   large
Mouquin's was a French restaurant better and more expensive
than the average. Mother discovered that the cheapest meal we
could get there was the dollar and twenty-five cent dinner. I
ordered one for each of us. She couldn't eat a morsel°. While the   mouthful, small bite
waiter served the courses and then removed her untouched plates
mother sat there and silently wept°.   cried

Later when mother's health was fading° I would bring her   failing; disappearing
flowers. It was no fun for either of us. No smile of pleasure would   slowly
light her face. She would shake her head in a pained way and
murmur, "They'll be dead in a day or two and a whole dollar
wasted." The uses of adversity° are not always sweet, Mr. Shake-   hard times
speare; they can be horrible and scarifying°.   frightening

When she died, mother left over five thousand dollars she had
scrimped together* somehow. She could have well spent this on
herself, but not with any pleasure. I can't say I learned the value of
money from my mother because I don't think she knew the value
of it. But my attitude toward money does stem from* her. I have
always followed the lesson she unwittingly° taught me: Spend It   unknowingly
While You Have It.

IDIOMS AND PHRASES*

coffee grounds	*particles that sink to the bottom*
chit of a child	*pert young girl*
subject to	*likely to get or have*
struck mother as	*seemed to be*
held her peace	*kept quiet*
held Dorothy's eye	*caught her attention*

high gear	*high speed*
high spirits	*good humor, happy state*
scrimped together	*saved*
stem from	*come from*

A

COMPREHENSION QUESTIONS

1. Why was Dorothy ill when her mother-in-law came to visit?

2. What does Mother do with her old coffee grounds?

3. In what way was Dorothy's appearance different from what her mother-in-law expected?

4. How did Mother show her approval of Dorothy?

5. Why did the author find it hard to treat his mother generously?

6. How did Mother react to the dinner at Mouquin's?

7. How did Mother feel about receiving flowers?

8. How much money did Mother leave after her death?

9. What did the author learn from his mother about money? Was this the lesson she intended to teach him?

B

VOCABULARY BUILDER

I. Match each word in the first column with the word or phrase in the second column that is closest to it in meaning.

1. confrontation
2. somewhat
3. lush
4. contracted
5. severe
6. hangover
7. wont
8. consequences
9. wisp
10. frugal
11. throb
12. submit
13. stammered

a. puzzled
b. state
c. tricks
d. celebration
e. luxuriant
f. pulse
g. in a way
h. economical
i. compressed
j. results
k. saved
l. large
m. hard times

14. bewildered
15. shifts (n.)
16. substantial
17. morsel
18. adversity
19. scrimped
20. unwittingly

n. effects of drinking too much alcohol
o. violent
p. unknowingly
q. custom
r. mouthful
s. meeting
t. small piece
u. spoke haltingly

II. Write sentences of your own using the underlined phrases.

Example: Jane's fear of the dark <u>stems from</u> her childhood.

The stain in the carpet <u>stems from</u> last night's party.

1. Jane was <u>subject to</u> fainting spells.

_____

2. Mary <u>held her peace</u> even though she disagreed with the speaker.

_____

3. He was in <u>high spirits</u> after he won the game.

_____

4. The comedians went into <u>high gear</u> in the second act.

_____

5. Their quarrel <u>stems from</u> school days.

_____

C

REVIEW OF IRREGULAR VERBS

Use the correct form of the irregular verb in parentheses.

Examples: If he _____ to Gibraltar, he will see many ships.
(go)

If he <u>goes</u> to Gibraltar, he will see many ships.

Last week, Mary ————————————————— beautifully.
(sing)
Last week, Mary sang beautifully.

Since he was ten, he ————————————————— English well.
(speak)
Since he was ten, he has spoken English well.

1. Last night he ————————————————— his mother out to dinner.
(take)

2. We went to many parties, which we knew ————————————————— Mother
(strike)
as an extravagance.

3. We had ————————————————— many songs before we left her apartment.
(sing)

4. Yesterday she ————————————————— the coffee grounds to her
(bring)
daughter-in-law's house.

5. Where have you ————————————————— the tools?
(hide)

6. We ————————————————— and ————————————————— all night
(drink)   (sing)
at the party.

7. "I ————————————————— you were going to mention that," he said to
(know)
his parents.

8. If you become a teacher, by your pupils you will be —————————————————.
(teach)

9. He ————————————————— the book on the floor because he was angry.
(fling)

10. The furniture ————————————————— when the train passed near the
(shake)
house.

11. Yesterday, after lunch, I ————————————————— down to take a nap.
(lie)

12. Where is the book that I ————————————————— on the table last week?
(lay)

13. Because of my cold, I have ————————————————— in this bed for four
(lie)
days.

14. I have ————————————————— you some gloves for your birthday.
(buy)

15. The ship _____ when it struck a reef.
(sink)

16. Please _____ down.
(lie)

17. _____ the rug under the glass table.
(Lay)

18. If you _____ down some firm rules, you will find that
(lay)
your pet will be easier to control.

19. She _____ in a deep sleep after a very exhausting day.
(lie)

20. _____ the packages on the table, and then go
(Lay)

_____ down to rest.
(lie)

D

WORD FORMS

Fill in the correct form of the words listed below.

1. confront, confronted, confronting, confrontation

   a. When she _____ him with the evidence, he
confessed his crime.

   b. There was a serious _____ between the two
nations.

   c. _____ Mary on the stairs, I demanded to know
where she had put my letter.

   d. When we _____ each other, I'm sure we shall
be able to come to an agreement.

2. sympathize, sympathized, sympathy, sympathetic, sympathetically

   a. Enid _____ with Larry when he told her about his
money problems.

   b. "I also get headaches, so I know how unpleasant it is," Mrs. Lindsay

murmured _____.

c. Mr. Lindsay was very ————————————— about Dorothy's hangover.

d. "I would like to ————————————— with you," the teacher stated to John, "but there is no excuse for forgetting to do your homework."

e. "Don't expect me to show you any ————————————— when you're not even trying to help yourself," Mother said to Dorothy.

3. ignore, ignored, ignoring, ignorance, ignorant

a. Because he was angry with her, he ————————————— her completely.

b. The best way to hide your ————————————— is to keep quiet.

c. Don't ————————————— your students when they want to ask questions; that is the only way they can learn.

d. I am totally ————————————— when it comes to gardening.

e. He was ————————————— the problem, hoping it would disappear.

E

PARALLEL STRUCTURE

1. Rewrite each of the following sentences according to the suggested pattern. Be sure that you have used parallel structure—that all the verbs are in the same tense and all the elements in the sentence have the same structure.

Example: Dorothy sat with us at the table, ate little, and contributed less to the conversation.

Dorothy was sitting with us at the table, was eating little, and was contributing less to the conversation.

a. They busily set up the screen, adjusted the projector, and sat down to watch the movie.

They were busily ————————————————————

——————————————————————————.

b. Jill admired her mother for her patience, diligence, and intelligence.

Jill admired her mother because she _____

_____.

c. The new principal promised to cut down class size, clean up the halls, and buy new teaching materials.

The new principal's promises included cutting down _____

_____.

d. The young boy loved to watch his father while he was shaving and dressing.

The young boy loved watching his father _____

_____.

2. Complete the following sentences by filling in the blanks.

Example: Some good things to eat are fish, _____, and breads.

 Some good things to eat are fish, <u>salads, and breads.</u>

a. Some good forms of exercise are <u>jogging,</u> _____,

and _____.

b. I enjoy <u>reading books,</u> _____and

_____.

c. We called the grocery store and ordered <u>flour,</u> _____,

and _____.

d. I want a house that has <u>a large kitchen,</u> _____,

and _____.

F

TOPICS FOR WRITING AND DISCUSSION

1. If the author felt the way his mother did about money, how would his style of life be different?

2. Did Mother's attitude toward money affect her ability to enjoy life? Is that always true? Why? Why not?

3. Mother spent a great deal of her life making economies. What are some of the ways by which you have learned to save money?

4. What advice about money would you give your children?

5. Describe a stingy person you have known. What were some of the unusual ways in which he or she economized?

6. Describe a spendthrift (a person who is careless about money) you have known. In what ways did he or she waste money?

The Romance of a Busy Broker

O. HENRY

O. Henry (1862–1910) was the pen name of William Sydney Porter. He wrote extremely popular stories dealing chiefly with the lives of ordinary people in large cities. The stories are marked by sentimentality and often by a surprise ending, which came to be known as the "O. Henry ending" and was widely imitated by other short-story writers. Collections of his stories include *Cabbages and Kings* (1904), *The Four Million* (1906), and *Waifs and Strays* (1917). O. Henry had a contract with the magazine of the *New York Sunday World* to write one story a week, at a rate of $100 per story, and it was a contract he managed to fulfill. In his early career he was a newspaperman and a bank clerk. He served a prison term in Ohio for stealing from the bank, although it is said that the bank's poor bookkeeping methods were responsible for the shortages of funds for which he was blamed.

Read the following selection, which is taken from *The Four Million*, for its overall effect. Don't stop to look up every word, but notice how the author builds up to his surprise ending. Then decide whether that ending makes the story more or less enjoyable.

PITCHER, CONFIDENTIAL CLERK* in the office of Harvey Maxwell, broker°, allowed a look of mild interest and surprise to visit his usually expressionless countenance° when his employer briskly entered at half-past nine in company with his young lady stenographer. With a snappy "Good-morning, Pitcher," Maxwell dashed at his desk as though he were intending to leap over it, and then plunged° into the great heap° of letters and telegrams waiting there for him.

 The young lady had been Maxwell's stenographer for a year. She was beautiful in a way that was decidedly° unstenographic. She forewent° the pomp° of the alluring pompadour°. She wore no chains, bracelets, or lockets. She had not the air of being about to accept an invitation to luncheon. Her dress was gray and plain, but it fitted her figure with fidelity° and discretion°. In her neat black turban hat was the gold-green wing of a macaw°. On this morning she was softly and shyly radiant°. Her eyes were dreamily bright, her cheeks genuine peach-blow, her expression a happy one, tinged° with reminiscence°.

 Pitcher, still mildly curious, noticed a difference in her ways

one who brings together buyers and sellers / face

dived / pile

definitely
refused / splendid display / woman's fancy hairdo
faithfulness / care

glowing

colored / remembrance

macaw

148

this morning. Instead of going straight into the adjoining room, where her desk was, she lingered°, slightly irresolute°, in the outer office. Once she moved over by Maxwell's desk, near enough for him to be aware of* her presence.

waited nearby / undecided

The machine sitting at that desk was no longer a man; it was a busy New York broker moved by buzzing wheels and uncoiling springs*.

"Well—what is it? Anything?" asked Maxwell, sharply. His opened mail lay like a bank° of stage snow* on his crowded desk. His keen° gray eye, impersonal and brusque°, flashed upon her half impatiently.

pile
sharp / quick

"Nothing," answered the stenographer, moving away with a little smile.

"Mr. Pitcher," she said to the confidential clerk, "did Mr. Maxwell say anything yesterday about engaging° another stenographer?"

hiring

"He did," answered Pitcher. "He told me to get another one. I notified the agency yesterday afternoon to send over a few samples this morning. It's 9.45 o'clock, and not a single picture hat or piece of pineapple chewing gum has showed up yet."

"I will do the work as usual, then," said the young lady, "until some one comes to fill the place." And she went to her desk at once and hung the black turban hat with the gold-green macaw wing in its accustomed° place.

usual

He who has been denied the spectacle° of a busy Manhattan broker during a rush of business is handicapped° for the profession of anthropology. The poet sings of the "crowded hour of glorious life." The broker's hour is not only crowded, but minutes and seconds are hanging to all the straps and packing both front and rear platforms.

sight
unequipped; crippled

And this day was Harvey Maxwell's busy day. The ticker° began to reel° out jerkily° its fitful° coils of tape, the desk telephone had a chronic° attack of buzzing. Men began to throng° into the office and call at him over the railing, jovially°, sharply, viciously°, excitedly. Messenger boys ran in and out with messages and telegrams. The clerks in the office jumped about like sailors during a storm. Even Pitcher's face relaxed into something resembling animation°.

machine that prints stock market transactions / wind / unevenly / in spurts / long-lasting / crowd / merrily / meanly

liveliness

On the Exchange* there were hurricanes° and landslides and snowstorms and glaciers° and volcanoes°, and those elemental disturbances were reproduced° in miniature in the broker's offices. Maxwell shoved° his chair against the wall and transacted business after the manner of a toe dancer. He jumped from ticker to 'phone, from desk to door with the trained agility° of a harlequin°.

sea storms
ice blocks / mountains with openings through which gases, etc., rise from below / copied / pushed / quickness / dancing clown

In the midst of this growing and important stress° the broker became suddenly aware of a high-rolled fringe° of golden hair under a nodding canopy° of velvet and ostrich° tips, an imitation sealskin sacque° and a string of beads as large as hickory nuts, ending near the floor with a silver heart. There was a self-possessed young lady connected with these accessories°, and Pitcher was there to construe° her.

"Lady from the Stenographer's Agency to see about the position," said Pitcher.

Maxwell turned half around, with his hands full of papers and ticker tape.

"What position?" he asked, with a frown°.

"Position of stenographer," said Pitcher. "You told me yesterday to call them up and have one sent over this morning."

"You are losing your mind, Pitcher," said Maxwell. "Why should I have given you any such instructions? Miss Leslie has given perfect satisfaction during the year she has been here. The place is hers as long as she chooses to retain° it. There's no place open here, madam. Countermand° that order with the agency, Pitcher, and don't bring any more of 'em in here."

The silver heart left the office, swinging and banging itself independently against the office furniture as it indignantly° departed. Pitcher seized a moment to remark to the bookkeeper that the "old man" seemed to get more absent-minded° and forgetful every day of the world.

The rush and pace of business grew fiercer° and faster. On the floor* they were pounding° half a dozen stocks in which Maxwell's customers were heavy investors. Orders to buy and sell were coming and going as swift° as the flight of swallows°. Some of his own holdings° were imperilled°, and the man was working like some high-geared°, delicate, strong machine—strung to full tension°, going at full speed, accurate, never hesitating, with the proper word and decision and act ready and prompt as clockwork. Stocks° and bonds°, loans and mortgages°, margins° and securities°—here was a world of finance, and there was no room in it for the human world or the world of nature.

When the luncheon hour drew near* there came a slight lull° in the uproar°.

Maxwell stood by his desk with his hands full of telegrams and memoranda, with a fountain pen over his right ear and his hair hanging in disorderly° strings over his forehead. His window was open, for the beloved janitress°, Spring, had turned on a little warmth through the waking registers° of the earth.

And through the window came a wandering—perhaps a

---

tension
trimming
overhanging covering /a
    large bird /short coat

ornamental extras
explain

displeased look

keep
take back, cancel

angrily

without thought for what
    one is doing
more violent
knocking down in price

fast /a type of bird
possessions /endangered
high-speed
stress; strain

shares in a company /
    certificates that promise
    interest on loaned
    money / loans made on
    property / part payments
    on stocks / stocks and
    bonds /period of
    quiet /outburst of noise
messy; confusing
cleaning woman
outlets for heating in a
    room

lost—odor—a delicate, sweet odor of lilac that fixed the broker for a moment immovable. For this odor belonged to Miss Leslie; it was her own, and hers only.

The odor brought her vividly°, almost tangibly° before him. The world of finance dwindled° suddenly to a speck°. And she was in the next room—twenty steps away.

clearly / able to be touched / became smaller / small spot

"By George, I'll do it now," said Maxwell, half aloud. "I'll ask her now. I wonder I didn't do it long ago."

He dashed into the inner office with the haste of a short trying to cover*. He charged° upon the desk of the stenographer.

came at high speed

She looked up at him with a smile. A soft pink crept over her cheek, and her eyes were kind and frank°. Maxwell leaned one elbow on her desk. He still clutched° fluttering° papers with both hands and the pen was above his ear.

open and honest

held tightly / windblown

"Miss Leslie," he began, hurriedly, "I have but a moment to spare. I want to say something in that moment. Will you be my wife? I haven't had time to make love to you in the ordinary way, but I really do love you. Talk quick, please—those fellows are clubbing the stuffing out of* Union Pacific°."

a railroad company

"Oh, what are you talking about?" exclaimed the young lady. She rose to her feet and gazed upon him, round-eyed.

"Don't you understand?" said Maxwell, restively°. "I want you to marry me. I love you, Miss Leslie. I wanted to tell you, and I snatched° a minute when things had slackened up* a bit. They're calling me for the 'phone now. Tell 'em to wait a minute, Pitcher. Won't you, Miss Leslie?"

impatiently

grabbed

The stenographer acted very queerly°. At first she seemed overcome with amazement°; then tears flowed from her wondering eyes; and then she smiled sunnily through them, and one of her arms slid tenderly° about the broker's neck.

strangely, oddly

great surprise

lovingly

"I know now," she said, softly. "It's this old business that has driven everything else out of your head for the time. I was frightened at first. Don't you remember, Harvey? We were married last evening at 8 o'clock in the Little Church around the Corner."

IDIOMS AND PHRASES*

confidential clerk	*private secretary*
to be aware of	*to sense, to know*
uncoiling springs	*unwinding wires*
stage snow	*artificial snow*
the Exchange	*New York Stock Exchange*
on the floor	*in the area (of the stock exchange) where business is done*

drew near	came closer
a short trying to cover	stock exchange term
clubbing the stuffing out of	beating
slackened up	slowed down

A

COMPREHENSION QUESTIONS

1. In what season of the year does the story take place?

2. Why is Harvey Maxwell so busy?

3. Were there real hurricanes, landslides, snowstorms, glaciers, and other elemental disturbances in the broker's office? What was really happening there and on the floor of the Exchange?

4. Compare the appearance of Miss Leslie and the young woman from the stenographers' agency.

5. How did Maxwell treat the woman from the stenographers' agency?

6. How much do you think Pitcher knows about the relationship between Mr. Maxwell and Miss Leslie?

7. Why does everyone assume that Miss Leslie has to leave her job?

8. What made Maxwell think of proposing?

9. What was Miss Leslie's reaction to Mr. Maxwell's second proposal?

10. Do you think it is possible that a man would forget he had been married the night before? Why?

B

VOCABULARY BUILDER

Answer the following questions briefly. You may have to consult a dictionary.

1. As <u>confidential clerk</u> to Mr. Maxwell, was Pitcher close to his boss?

2. Why was Pitcher's <u>countenance</u> usually expressionless?

3. Is the stenographer's <u>adjoining</u> room near to or far from Mr. Maxwell's office? Is that her <u>accustomed</u> place?

4. The stenographer <u>lingered</u> slightly <u>irresolute.</u> What was she doing?

5. Is a bed with <u>uncoiling springs</u> comfortable?

6. Is a keen look, <u>impersonal</u> and <u>brusque,</u> a very friendly look? Why or why not?

7. When you are <u>engaging</u> another stenographer, do you give her a diamond ring?

8. Is a <u>chronic</u> attack sudden? Can you prepare for it?

9. Why does the ticker <u>jerkily reel out</u> <u>fitful</u> coils of tape? Does it behave the same way when there are just a few stock prices to be reported?

10. Mr. Maxwell has the <u>agility</u> of a harlequin. Does he move slowly?

11. Have you ever been asked to <u>construe</u> a passage in a book? How is it done?

12. Give an antonym for <u>frown.</u>

13. How is your life <u>imperilled</u> if you drive too fast?

14. How did the stenographer who <u>indignantly departed</u> leave the office?

15. What is an <u>absent-minded</u> professor?

16. Do you like people who are <u>prompt</u>? Why?

17. Is the lunchtime <u>lull</u> in the <u>uproar</u> temporary or permanent? Do things <u>slacken up</u> a bit?

18. Is a <u>disorderly</u> office neat?

19. When you have a <u>frank</u> talk with a friend, do you discuss things openly, or do you keep secrets from each other?

20. Is <u>countermanding</u> an order a sign of approval?

C
ADJECTIVES

Form adjectives by using the suffix **-ous, -y, -ic, -ed,** or **-ing** with each of the underlined words below.

Examples: an experiment in <u>science</u>   **a <u>scientific</u> experiment**

   a book of <u>interest</u>   **an <u>interesting</u> book**

1. a speech that <u>bores</u>   _____ speech

2. a story of <u>romance</u>   _____ story

3. hair full of <u>curls</u>   _____ hair

4. child with a <u>handicap</u>   _____ child

5. a letter of <u>sympathy</u>   _____ letter

6. a man full of <u>pomp</u>   _____ man

7. a couple full of <u>charm</u>   _____ couple

8. a face with a <u>smile</u> _____ face

9. eyes full of <u>wonder</u> _____ eyes

10. glance of <u>fascination</u> _____ glance

11. manner full of <u>mystery</u> _____ manner

12. a look of <u>love</u> _____ look

13. a sound full of <u>vibrations</u> _____ sound

14. look of <u>anger</u> _____ look

15. a situation filled with <u>danger</u> _____ situation

16. desire to <u>poison</u> _____ desire

17. a laugh of <u>joy</u> _____ laugh

18. a hostess with <u>grace</u> _____ hostess

19. a book of <u>tragedy</u> _____ book

20. a feeling of <u>guilt</u> _____ feeling

D

TRANSITIONAL DEVICES

Transitional devices connect ideas, sentences, and paragraphs. They make writing more unified and clear. Some words used as transitional devices are **afterward, however, then, and, but, as soon as, consequently, another, therefore, at first,** and **as a result.**

1. In the paragraph that follows, fill in the appropriate transitional words from the list above.

On Monday, John bought one hundred shares of common

stock. _____ the price of the stock

started to go up. _____, John wanted

to sell the stock when it was two dollars higher than his

original cost, _____ he became

greedy _____ he decided to hold on to

the stock for _____ few days. He

_____ gave orders to his stockbroker to

hold the stock for _____ month.

_____ John left for his vacation.

_____ he left, the price of the stock began to

fall. The broker tried to reach John, _____

couldn't. _____, John lost all his money.

_____ of his experience, John learned

not to be greedy.

2. Write a paragraph entitled "My Most Embarrassing Moment." Use as many of these transitional devices as you can: **finally, furthermore, still, yet, and, but, then, later, meanwhile, at the same time, for this reason, next.**

E

CONDITIONAL: UNREAL

One type of conditional statement describes a situation in which the condition is unreal (is untrue or has not happened). It is expressed by using the simple past tense in the **if** clause and **would, could,** or **might** plus the simple form of the verb in the **result** clause.

1. Change the following sentences to present unreal conditional statements.

Example: If I study, I will pass the test.

　　　　　If I **studied,** I **would pass** the test.

　　a. If he leaves, we will know it.

　　b. If you come late, I won't wait for you.

   c. I'll call you if I see Mother.

   d. If it snows, we'll go skiing.

   e. If the radio breaks, Susan won't hear her favorite program.

   f. If the stenographer retires, you will get the job.

   g. I'll walk to the park if the weather is nice.

   h. If she loves me, I'll propose to her.

   i. If the clock runs quietly, I'll buy it.

   j. If there is an earthquake, the town will be destroyed.

2. Make up ten unreal conditional statements of your own, making sure that you use the simple past tense in the **if** clause and **would** plus the simple form of the verb in the **result** clause.

F

TOPICS FOR WRITING AND DISCUSSION

1. Harvey Maxwell deals in stocks, bonds, mortgages, margins, and securities. What are the differences between these things?

2. Mr. Maxwell's proposal is very unusual. Suggest a more romantic setting and approach.

3. Compare the advantages and disadvantages of investing in the stock market with the advantages and disadvantages of keeping your money in the bank.

4. What factors drive the prices of stocks up and down?

5. Write a paragraph describing someone you know or have read about who is as totally involved in his or her business or work as is Mr. Maxwell. How have that individual's personal relationships been affected?

University Days

PART I

JAMES THURBER

James Thurber (1894–1961) is considered the best American humor writer since Mark Twain. He is known for the irony, satire, and whimsical humor of his stories about ordinary American life. He is also known for his masterful cartoons. Thurber lost one eye in a childhood accident, but despite that and the gradual weakening of the other eye over the years, he had a very successful writing career, contributing hundreds of stories, articles, and cartoons to *The New Yorker*. Some of his stories have been made into films, most notably "The Secret Life of Walter Mitty," the film version of which starred Danny Kaye. Thurber's books include *My Life and Hard Times* (1933), from which this story is taken, and *My World and Welcome to It* (1942).

"University Days" is based on the author's experiences as a student at Ohio State University, which he left in 1918. It is one of the most popular of all his stories. The accompanying drawings are also Thurber's.

I PASSED° ALL THE OTHER COURSES that I took at my University, but I could never pass botany. This was because all botany students had to spend several hours a week in a laboratory looking through a microscope at plant cells°, and I could never see through a microscope. I never once saw a cell through a microscope. This used to enrage° my instructor. He would wander around the laboratory pleased with the progress all the students were making in drawing the involved and, so I am told, interesting structure of flower cells, until he came to me. I would just be standing there. "I can't see anything," I would say. He would begin patiently enough, explaining how anybody can see through a microscope, but he would always end up in a fury°, claiming

was examined in a course of study and went on to the next course / units of living matter

anger

rage, extreme anger

157

that I could *too* see through a microscope but just pretended that I couldn't. "It takes away from the beauty of flowers anyway," I used to tell him. "We are not concerned with beauty in this course," he would say. "We are concerned solely° with what I may call the *mechanics°* of flars°." "Well," I'd say, "I can't see anything." "Try it just once again," he'd say, and I would put my eye to the microscope and see nothing at all, except now and again a nebulous° milky substance—a phenomenon° of maladjustment°. You were supposed to see a vivid, restless clockwork of sharply defined plant cells. "I see what looks like a lot of milk," I would tell him. This, he claimed, was the result of my not having adjusted° the microscope properly, so he would readjust it for me, or rather, for himself. And I would look again and see milk.

I finally took a deferred° pass, as they called it, and waited a year and tried again. (You had to pass one of the biological sciences or you couldn't graduate.) The professor had come back from vacation brown as a berry, bright-eyed, and eager to explain cell-structure again to his classes. "Well," he said to me, cheerily, when we met in the first laboratory hour of the semester°, "we're going to see cells this time, aren't we?" "Yes, sir," I said. Students to right of me and to left of me and in front of me were seeing cells; what's more*, they were quietly drawing pictures of them in their notebooks. Of course, I didn't see anything

"We'll try it," the professor said to me, grimly°," with every adjustment of the microscope known to man. As God is my witness, I'll arrange this glass so that you see cells through it or I'll give up* teaching. In twenty-two years of botany, I—" He cut off abruptly for he was beginning to quiver all over, like Lionel Barrymore, and he genuinely wished to hold onto his temper*, his scenes with me had taken a great deal out of him.

So we tried it with every adjustment of the microscope known to man. With only one of them did I see anything but blackness or the familiar lacteal° opacity°, and that time I saw, to my pleasure and amazement, a variegated° constellation° of flecks, specks,° and dots. These I hastily drew. The instructor, noting my activity, came back from an adjoining° desk, a smile on his lips and his eyebrows high in hope. He looked at my cell drawing. "What's that?" he demanded, with a hint° of a squeal° in his voice. "That's what I saw," I said. "You didn't, you didn't, you *did*n't!" he screamed, losing control of his temper instantly, and he bent over and squinted° into the microscope. His head snapped up. "That's your eye!" he shouted. "You've fixed the lens so that it reflects! You've drawn your eye!"

Another course that I didn't like, but somehow managed to

only

science of motion and
force / flowers

cloudlike; indistinct /
remarkable or unusual
thing / faulty
adjustment

focused; corrected

postponed

division of a university
year

sternly

milky / opaque quality
marked with different-
colored patches / group
of fixed stars / small spots
of dirt or color / nearby

slight suggestion or
indication / shrill sound
indicating pain

looked with half-shut
eyes

He was beginning to quiver all over, like Lionel Barrymore.

pass, was economics. I went to that class straight from the botany class, which didn't help me any in understanding either subject. I used to get them mixed up. But not as mixed up as another student in my economics class who came there direct from a physics laboratory. He was a tackle° on the football team, named Bolenciecwcz. At that time Ohio State University had one of the best football teams in the country, and Bolenciecwcz was one of its outstanding stars. In order to be eligible° to play it was necessary for him to keep up* in his studies, a very difficult matter, for while he was not dumber than an ox he was not any smarter. Most of his professors were lenient° and helped him along. None gave him more hints, in answering questions, or asked him simpler ones than the economics professor, a thin, timid man named Bassum. One day when we were on the subject of transportation and distribution, it came Bolenciecwcz's turn to answer a question. "Name one means of transportation," the professor said to him. No light came into the big tackle's eyes. "Just any means of transportation," said the professor. Bolenciecwcz sat staring at him. "That is," pursued the professor, "any medium, agency, or method of going from one place to another." Bolenciecwcz had

a football player in a specific position on the line of scrimmage

fit

understanding

the look of a man who is being led into a trap. "You may choose among steam, horse-drawn, or electrically propelled° vehicles," driven forward said the instructor. "I might suggest the one which we commonly take in making long journeys across land." There was a profound° deep silence in which everybody stirred° uneasily, including Bolen- moved ciecwcz and Mr. Bassum. Mr. Bassum abruptly broke this silence in an amazing manner. "Choo-choo-choo," he said, in a low voice, and turned instantly scarlet°. He glanced appealingly bright red around the room. All of us, of course, shared Mr. Bassum's desire that Bolenciecwcz should stay abreast of* the class in economics, for the Illinois game, one of the hardest and most important of the season, was only a week off. "Toot, toot, too-tooooooot!" some student with a deep voice moaned, and we all looked encourag- ingly at Bolenciecwcz. Somebody else gave a fine imitation of a locomotive letting off steam. Mr. Bassum himself rounded off* the little show. "Ding, dong, ding, dong," he said, hopefully. Bolenciecwcz was staring at the floor now, trying to think, his great brow furrowed°, his huge hands rubbing together, his face lined red.

Bolenciecwcz was trying to think.

"How did you come to college this year, Mr. Bolenciecwcz?" asked the professor. "*Chuffa* chuffa, *chuffa* chuffa."

"M'father sent me," said the football player.

"What on?" asked Bassum.

"I git an 'lowance°," said the tackle, in a low, husky voice, obviously embarrassed.

allowance: an amount of money given to someone regularly

"No, no," said Bassum. "Name a means of transportation. What did you *ride* here on?"

"Train," said Bolenciecwcz.

"Quite right," said the professor. "Now, Mr. Nugent, will you tell us——"

IDIOMS AND PHRASES*

what's more	*in addition*
give up	*leave*
hold onto his temper	*not become angry*
keep up	*continue*
stay abreast of	*keep up with*
rounded off	*finished*

A

COMPREHENSION QUESTIONS

1. What does the author usually see in the microscope instead of flower cells?

2. Why did the author take botany over again?

3. When the author finally did see something different in the microscope, what was it?

4. Why did the botany teacher lose his temper?

5. What other class besides botany did the author dislike?

6. What college did the author attend?

7. What position did Bolenciecwcz play on the football team?

8. Why was it important to help Bolenciecwcz pass his courses?

9. What did a train have to do with economics?

10. How did Bolenciecwcz finally arrive at the right answer?

B

VOCABULARY BUILDER

I. Match the words in the first column with their meanings in the second column.

1. furrowed	**a.** slight suggestion
2. allowance	**b.** shrill sound
3. propelled	**c.** looked with half-shut eyes
4. stirred	**d.** football player
5. scarlet	**e.** understanding
6. hint	**f.** driven forward
7. lenient	**g.** moved
8. eligible	**h.** bright red
9. tackle	**i.** amount of money given regularly
10. squeal	**j.** fit
11. squinted	**k.** lined

II. Match the synonyms below.

1. nebulous	**a.** corrected
2. adjusted	**b.** delayed
3. deferred	**c.** indistinct
4. semester	**d.** term
5. grimly	**e.** sternly
6. lacteal	**f.** dullness
7. opacity	**g.** spots
8. specks	**h.** milky

III. Make sentences using the following phrases.

1. hold onto his temper

2. stay abreast of

3. rounded off

University Days
PART II

I F I WENT THROUGH ANGUISH° in botany and economics—for different reasons—gymnasium work* was even worse. I don't even like to think about it. They wouldn't let you play games or join in the exercises with your glasses on and I couldn't see with mine off. I bumped into professors, horizontal bars, agricultural students, and swinging° iron rings. Not being able to see, I could take it* but I couldn't dish it out*. Also, in order to pass gymnasium (and you had to pass it to graduate) you had to learn to swim if you didn't know how. I didn't like the swimming pool, I didn't like swimming, and I didn't like the swimming instructor, and after all these years I still don't. I never swam but I passed my gym work anyway, by having another student give my gymnasium number (978) and swim across the pool in my place. He was a quiet, amiable blonde youth, number 473, and he would have seen through a microscope for me if we could have got away with it*, but we couldn't get away with it. Another thing I didn't like about gymnasium work was that they made you strip° the day you registered. It is impossible for me to be happy when I am stripped and being asked a lot of questions. Still, I did better than a lanky° agricultural student who was cross-examined° just before I was. They asked each student what college° he was in—that is, whether Arts, Engineering, Commerce, or Agriculture. "What college are you in?" the instructor snapped at the youth in front of me. "Ohio State University," he said promptly.

It wasn't that agricultural student but it was another a whole lot* like him who decided to take up* journalism, possibly on the ground° that when farming went to hell* he could fall back on* newspaper work. He didn't realize, of course, that that would be very much like falling back full-length° on a kit° of carpenter's tools. Haskins didn't seem cut out* for journalism, being too embarrassed to talk to anybody and unable to use a typewriter, but the editor of the college paper assigned him to the cow barns, the sheep house, the horse pavilion, and the animal husbandry° de-

severe suffering

moving backward and forward

take off one's clothes

tall and lean / questioned closely / school of higher education; a part of a university

reason for saying, doing, or believing something

completely / set

farming

partment generally. This was a genuinely big "beat°," for it took
up five times as much ground and got ten times as great a legisla-
tive appropriation* as the College of Liberal Arts. The agricultural
student knew animals, but nevertheless° his stories were dull and
colorlessly written. He took all afternoon on each of them, on
account of* having to hunt for* each letter on the typewriter. Once
in a while* he had to ask somebody to help him hunt. "C" and
"L," in particular, were hard letters for him to find. His editor
finally got pretty much annoyed at the farmer-journalist because
his pieces° were so uninteresting. "See here, Haskins," he
snapped at him one day, "Why is it we never have anything hot°
from you on the horse pavilion? Here we have two hundred head of
horses on this campus—more than any other university in the
Western Conference except Purdue—and yet you never get any real
low down* on them. Now shoot over* to the horse barns and dig up*
something lively." Haskins shambled out and came back in about
an hour; he said he had something. "Well, start it off snappily°,"
said the editor. "Something people will read." Haskins set to work
and in a couple of hours brought a sheet of typewritten paper to the
desk; it was a two-hundred word story about some disease that had
broken out among the horses. Its opening sentence was simple but
arresting°. It read: "Who has noticed the sores° on the tops of the
horses in the animal husbandry building?"

Ohio State was a land grant* university and therefore two
years of military drill* was compulsory°. We drilled with old
Springfield rifles and studied the tactics of the Civil War even
though the World War was going on at the time. At 11 o'clock
each morning thousands of freshmen and sophomores* used to
deploy° over the campus, moodily creeping up on the old chemis-
try building. It was good training for the kind of warfare that was
waged° at Shiloh° but it had no connection with what was going
on in Europe. Some people used to think there was German
money behind it, but they didn't dare° say so or they would have
been thrown in jail as German spies. It was a period of muddy°
thought and marked, I believe, the decline of higher education in
the Middle West.

As a soldier I was never any good at all. Most of the cadets°
were glumly° indifferent° soldiers, but I was no good at all. Once
General Littlefield, who was commandant of the cadet corps,
popped up* in front of me during regimental drill and snapped,
"You are the main trouble with this university!" I think he meant
that my type was the main trouble with the university but he
may have meant me individually. I was mediocre° at drill,

Marginal glosses (right column):

- beat° — area of responsibility
- nevertheless° — yet, still
- pieces° — writings
- hot° — new; impressive
- snappily° — in a lively manner
- arresting° — attention-catching / sores° — painful spots
- compulsory° — must be done
- deploy° — spread out in line of battle
- waged° — carried on / Shiloh° — Civil War battleground
- dare° — have the courage to / muddy° — unclear
- cadets° — students taking military training / glumly° — sadly / indifferent° — uncaring
- mediocre° — not very good, second-rate

certainly—that is, until my senior year. By that time I had drilled longer than anybody else in the Western Conference, having failed° at military at the end of each preceding° year so that I had to do it all over again. I was the only senior still in uniform. The uniform which, when new, had made me look like an interurban° railway conductor, now that it had become faded and too tight made me look like Bert Williams° in his bellboy° act. This had a definitely bad effect on my morale°. Even so, I had become by sheer° practise little short of wonderful at squad manoeuvres°.

°been unsuccessful / the one before

°connecting cities

°an actor / someone employed by a hotel to carry luggage / confidence / thorough / military movements (British spelling)

One day General Littlefield picked our company out of the whole regiment and tried to get it mixed up by putting it through one movement after another as fast as we could execute° them: squads right, squads left, squads on right into line, squads right about, squads left front into line, etc. In about three minutes one hundred and nine men were marching in one direction and I was marching away from them at an angle of forty degrees, all alone. "Company, halt!" shouted General Littlefield. "That man is the only man who has it right!" I was made a corporal for my achievement.

°do

The next day General Littlefield summoned° me to his office. He was swatting° flies when I went in. I was silent and he was silent too, for a long time. I don't think he remembered me or why he had sent for me, but he didn't want to admit it. He swatted some more flies, keeping his eyes on them narrowly before he let go* with the swatter. "Button up your coat!" he snapped. Looking back on it now I can see that he meant me although he was looking at a fly, but I just stood there. Another fly came to rest on a paper in front of the general and began rubbing its hind° legs together. The general lifted the swatter cautiously. I moved restlessly and the fly flew away. "You startled° him!" barked General Littlefield, looking at me severely. I said I was sorry. "That won't help the situation!" snapped the General, with cold military logic. I didn't see what I could do except offer to chase some more flies toward his desk, but I didn't say anything. He stared out the window at the faraway° figures of co-eds crossing the campus toward the library. Finally, he told me I could go. So I went. He either didn't know which cadet I was or else he forgot what he wanted to see me about. It may have been that he wished to apologize for having called me the main trouble with the university; or maybe he had decided to compliment me on my brilliant drilling of the day before and then at the last minute decided not to. I don't know. I don't think about it much any more.

°called

°hitting with a sharp blow

°back

°caused to move or jump

°distant

IDIOMS AND PHRASES*

gymnasium work	*physical training*
take it	*bear trouble*
dish it out	*treat someone roughly*
got away with it	*done it without being caught or punished*
whole lot	*very much*
take up	*begin to do, or learn*
went to hell	*became ruined*
fall back on	*turn to, rely on*
cut out	*suited*
legislative appropriation	*money given by the government for a specific purpose*
on account of	*because of*
hunt for	*look for*
once in a while	*occasionally*
low down	*facts*
shoot over	*hurry*
dig up	*find; get*
land grant	*public land allotted by the government*
military drill	*army training*
freshmen and sophomores	*first- and second-year students*
popped up	*appeared suddenly*
let go	*attacked*

A

COMPREHENSION QUESTIONS

1. Why did the author dislike gymnasium?

2. How did he pass his swimming test?

3. Why couldn't he pass botany the same way?

4. Does the author think highly of the agriculture students at the college? How can you tell?

5. Why was Haskins unsuited for journalism?

6. What was Haskins's arresting story? Was it really startling?

7. What is a land grant university?

8. Why was the author such a poor soldier?

9. Did the author think the military drills were very useful?

10. How did the author get a promotion in the military?

11. Do you think the author was a poor student? Why?

12. Do you get the impression that the author liked school?

B

VOCABULARY BUILDER

I. In your own words, describe the words below.

1. gymnasium
2. manoeuvres
3. bellboy

4. cadets
5. military drill

II. Match the words in the first column with their antonyms in the second column.

1. startled
2. hind
3. preceding
4. mediocre
5. muddy
6. compulsory
7. lanky
8. strip
9. swinging
10. anguish

a. front
b. following
c. contentment
d. still
e. stocky, stout
f. dress
g. voluntary
h. clear
i. first-rate
j. unsurprised

C

IDIOMS

Fill in the blanks with the phrase from the story that means the same thing as the words in parentheses.

1. He can _____, but not very graciously.
                      (bear trouble)

2. Having _____ business, he
                  (been unsuccessful at)

_____ medicine.
          (tried)

3. Don't _____ unless you can stand criticism in return.
(treat roughly)

4. She thought she could _____, but her blushes gave her
(do it without being caught)
away.

5. He _____ at our house whenever he was in the mood.
(appeared suddenly)

6. "_____ to the store," Mother said, "and pick up some
(Hurry over)
milk."

7. Give me the _____ on the new kind of engine.
(facts)

8. They were late _____ the baby sitter.
(because of)

9. _____, I manage to guess which stock to buy.
(Occasionally)

10. Some women are not _____ for modeling.
(suited)

11. I can always _____ teaching.
(turn to)

12. He pleaded innocent to the charge, _____ it was
(for the reason that)
self-defense.

13. This sounds _____ like a story I read in the newspaper.
(very much)

14. She had to _____ a pen in the desk drawer.
(find)

15. "I'll try to _____ that information for you," the librarian
(find)
said.

D

WORD FORMS

Fill in the correct form of the words listed below.

1. explain, explained, explaining, explanation

   a. He would begin by _____ that anybody could pass
botany if he could see through a microscope.

b. His ——————————————— of transportation and distribution was very complicated.

c. Please ——————————————— why you are so late for class.

d. She ——————————————— that she was very serious about passing economics.

2. adjust, adjusted, adjusting, adjustment

a. ——————————————— the microscope in order to see plant cells was very difficult for the botany student.

b. The professor ——————————————— the microscope, but I could see only a milky substance.

c. He quickly ——————————————— to university life.

d. Becoming a student of economics was a difficult ——————————————— for Bolenciecwcz.

e. When you live with others in the same house, you must learn to

——————————————— your schedule to theirs.

3. demand, demanded, demanding

a. There is a great ——————————————— for capable scientists.

b. Mr. Bassum, the economics professor, was very lenient and not

———————————————.

c. He ——————————————— that I show him my homework.

d. He was ——————————————— that we all write articles for the school newspaper.

4. arrange, arranged, arranging, arrangements

a. If you don't do your work, I shall ——————————————— that you fail the course.

b. All the ——————————————— for the party were made by the students.

c. He ——————————————— to let her take the swimming test
again.

d. ——————————————— the schedule took all her energy.

E

COURSES OF STUDY

Fill in the profession or occupation that matches the course of study listed in the first
column.

Example: If you study <u>typing,</u> you will become a ———————————————.

      If you study <u>typing,</u> you will become a <u>typist</u>.

If you study	*you will become a*
1. law	————————————————
2. medicine	————————————————
3. journalism	————————————————
4. accounting	————————————————
5. biology	————————————————
6. chemistry	————————————————
7. economics	————————————————
8. psychology	————————————————
9. art	————————————————
10. music	————————————————
11. geology	————————————————
12. engineering	————————————————
13. physics	————————————————

14. drama   _____

15. pharmacology   _____

16. architecture   _____

17. philosophy   _____

18. history   _____

19. mathematics   _____

20. languages   _____

F

CONDITIONAL: PAST UNREAL

In a past statement in which the condition is unreal or untrue, we use the past perfect tense in the **if** clause and **would have**, **could have**, or **might have** plus the past participle in the **result** clause.

Example: If it _____ yesterday, Mary
                                    (snow)

_____boots.
                    (wear)
If it <u>had snowed</u> yesterday, Mary <u>would have worn</u> boots.

If I _____ to class, I
                        (not go)

_____that player.
                    (not meet)
If I <u>had not gone</u> to class, I <u>would not have met</u> that player.

Change the following sentences to past unreal conditional statements. Make sure you use the correct form of the verb in parentheses.

1. If Edna _____ to Europe last summer, she
                        (not go)

_____ John.
                (not meet)

2. If I _____ enough money, I
                    (have)

_____ a microscope.
                (buy)

3. If the agricultural student ————————————— how to
(know)

type well, he ————————————— his stories faster.
(write)

4. If Haskins ————————————— up something lively, he
(dig)

————————————— it published.
(get)

5. Thurber ————————————— university life if he
(enjoy)

————————————— to participate in military drill.
(not have)

6. If I ————————————— at military, I
(not fail)

————————————— it again the following year.
(not take)

7. If General Littlefield ————————————— why he had sent
(not forget)

for me, he ————————————— my military skill.
(praise)

8. If she ————————————— up her coat, she
(button)

————————————— warm.
(feel)

9. If James ————————————— his schedule properly, he
(arrange)

————————————— all his work on time.
(finish)

10. If the weather —————————————, we
(not improve)

————————————— on a picnic.
(not go)

11. If Thurber ————————————— his class standing, he
(not maintain)

————————————— to leave the university.
(have)

12. We ————————————— the soldiers pass by if we
(see)

————————————— near the corner.
(stand)

13. If your eyesight ————————————— good, you
(be)

————————————— glasses.
(not need)

14. I ———————————————— you if I
$\qquad$ (call)

———————————————— your telephone number.
$\qquad$ (know)

15. If I ———————————————— able to swim, I
$\qquad$ (be)

———————————————— the test.
$\qquad$ (pass)

G

TOPICS FOR WRITING AND DISCUSSION

1. Describe some amusing events that have happened to you or around you in school.

2. What courses do you dislike the most in school, and why?

3. Do you believe that some people actually have learning blocks in certain subjects—in mathematics or foreign languages, for example? Why? Why not? Defend your opinion with specific examples.

4. Are there any specific courses or procedures that you would like to see changed in your school? Is there anything that seems particularly silly or unreasonable? Explain fully.

5. Compare the advantages and disadvantages of a university education with the advantages and disadvantages of studying for a trade.

GLOSSARY

The glossary that follows contains the words and expressions that are defined either in the marginal glosses or the Idioms and Phrases following each reading. They are accompanied by page references, enabling students to readily locate new vocabulary in this alphabetical listing and in its original context. Slang expressions and words that are archaic or infrequently used have been omitted. Where there might be some confusion, we have repeated the definition or indicated the form of the word with the following abbreviations: *adj.* = adjective; *adv.* = adverb; *n.* = noun; *v.* = verb.

abandon(ed), *v.*, 55
abandoned, *adj.*, 97
aboard, 55
about to, 40, 65
abruptly, 108
absentminded, 150
absorbing:
   completely taking up
   the attention or thoughts,
   129
accessories, 150
according to, 15
accustomed, *adj.*, 149
addiction, 26
adjoining, 159
adjust, 158
adventuress, 54
adversity, 139
afford, *v.*, 99
agility, 149
agony, 110
alarm, *n.*, 40
all told, 15
allowance, 160
amazement, 151
amiable, 54
anguish, 169
animation, 149
annoy(ed), 27, 85

annoyance, 77
apologetic, 54
apprehensively, 98
arresting:
   attention-getting, 164
as a matter of fact, 27
ass: donkey, 129
associate, *n.*, 27
assume(d), 27
assured, *adj.*, 26
assuredly, 77
astonished, *adj.*, 42
at length, 109
at the outside, 28
attract attention, 119
attractive, 54
audition, *n.*, 100
awful, *adj.*, 40
awfully, 108
awkward, 128

backed her up, 99
backyard, 76
bank, *n.*: pile, 149
baton(s), 97
beat, *n.*:
   area of responsibility, 164
be aware of, 149
bellboy, 165

bent on, 14
bewildered, *adj.*, 139
bill of fare, 128
bird in the hand is worth
   two in the bush, a, 76
blasphemy, 3
blessed, *adj.*, 26
board:
   meals by the week
   or month, 109
bobby pin(s), 94
bond(s), 150
boundless, *adj.*, 64
brace, *v.*, 108
brand-new, 65
broken-hearted, 109
broker, 147
brusque, 149
buckskin, 128
bumper(s), 76
bump into, 54

cadet(s), 164
call(ed) up, 3
call on, 108
canopy, 150
canter(ing), *v.*, 95
care, *n.*, 85
carve, 65

ANSWER KEY

COMPLAINT DEPARTMENT

B 1. transacts 2. nature 3. readjustment 4. perspiration 5. desolately 6. state
7. resorted to 8. blasphemy 9. writhed 10. reminiscence 11. crawly, worms
12. I beg your pardon 13. It's like this

D 1. a. connection b. connect c. connecting
2. a. transact b. transaction c. transacting
3. a. wrapping, wrap b. Wrap c. wraps, wrapper d. wrapping (wrapper)
e. wrapping

E 1. isn't he 2. isn't she 3. weren't we 4. aren't they 5. wasn't I 6. won't you
7. can't you 8. aren't you 9. weren't you 10. won't we

F 1. said 2. told 3. told 4. told, said 5. said 6. told 7. tell 8. tell 9. say
10. say 11. tells 12. tell 13. say 14. tell 15. said

G 1. go 2. went 3. goes, will buy 4. bought 5. takes 6. was taking 7. Drive
8. driving 9. drove 10. left 11. leave 12. was leaving 13. think 14. thought
15. thinking 16. give 17. gave 18. will give 19. See 20. saw. 21. shall see

H 1. Jamie asked his mother to give him more candy.
2. Mother said that it's not good for you.
3. Mr. Seeley told the operator that he wished to register a complaint.
4. She said that she would connect him with the complaint department.
5. Mr. Seeley said that there were worms in his flour.
6. Lois said that she always lets people get ahead of her on checkout lines in the supermarket.
7. The tour guide advised the tourists to get to the bus early to be sure to get a seat.
8. The zoo keeper warned him not to approach the gorilla because the gorilla might grab his tie.
9. The doctor told his patient that running is a good form of exercise.
10. Mr. Seeley complained to the manager that the operator was very uncooperative.
1. a. I beg your pardon. I didn't mean to step on your toes.
   b. I beg your pardon. I didn't mean to hurt your feelings.
   c. I beg your pardon. I didn't mean to take your pencil.
2. a. I want to tell you about my boyfriend.
   b. I want to tell you about my meeting with John.
   c. I want to tell you about my problem with the complaint department.
3. a. They could hardly wait to see Jane.
   b. We could hardly wait for the delivery of our new rings.
   c. I can hardly wait to see how the new coat I bought for Tommy fits him.

THE TIME KILLER

B   1. h 2. c 3. b 4. e 5. a 6. g 7. d 8. j 9. i 10. f

D   1. Will it take about an hour to explain this to you?
2. Does it have to be done?
3. Can you go to American Express for your mail?
4. Did I look at the list of arrivals?
5. Does he have to speak to you even if he doesn't know you?

E   1. killed 2. went 3. found 4. spoke 5. interfered 6. thought, would
7. stopped, picked 8. printed 9. took 10. did

F   1. a. reporting b. reporter c. report
2. a. interference b. interfere c. interfering
3. a. discussing b. discussing c. discussion
4. a. distinctly b. distinct c. distinction
5. a. known b. Knowing c. knowledge d. know

G   1. claims 2. called 3. did, live 4. worked 5. moved 6. spelled 7. worked
8. plays 9. moved 10. lived, visited 11. killed 12. discussed 13. stayed
14. sulks

H   1. into 2. to 3. out of 4. out of 5. toward 6. away from 7. toward 8. to
9. into 10. out of, into

I   an, a, the, the, a, a, an

J   1. asking 2. fishing 3. studying 4. coming 5. calling 6. falling 7. running
8. lying 9. hunting 10. dying 11. getting 12. having 13. appearing
14. knowing 15. finding 16. traveling 17. letting 18. driving 19. taking
20. putting

THE LATE MR. ADAMS

B   1. seriously 2. very bad habits 3. on purpose 4. fellow worker 5. strolled
6. possibility 7. good qualities 8. important 9. came together 10. accepted
11. calmly 12. bad habit 13. cleaning man 14. accident 15. go to bed
16. late 17. turning 18. university administrator 19. business administrators
20. shiny

D   1. us (object) 2. us (object) 3. who (subject) 4. who (subject) 5. I (subject)
6. me (object) 7. she (subject) 8. who (subject) 9. him (object) 10. them (object)

E   1. His father gave him the impression that he would be promoted.
2. George's lateness drove her to tears.
3. George reserved the honeymoon suite.
4. His mother weaned him late.
5. The family decided that all the other cars should proceed as planned.
6. I washed my car last week.
7. Cathy considers this the best watch you can buy.
8. A famous French historian wrote the book.

9. Labor and management reached an agreement.
10. The baby sitter bathed and fed the baby before he was put to bed.
11. Two people produced the program.

F 1. a 2. — 3. — 4. the 5. a 6. The, — 7. — 8. —, a 9. a 10. the, —
11. a 12. a 13. The, — 14. — 15. —

G 1. in 2. On 3. to 4. at 5. in 6. next to 7. at 8. After 9. on 10. to 11. in
12. from 13. until

H 1. realized, had taken 2. left, had typed 3. had been married, had 4. wanted, had
bought 5. had never been, sailed 6. never received, had ordered 7. remembered,
had taken 8. had reserved, arrived 9. continued, had reduced 10. played, had
stopped 11. was, had expected 12. got, had already started 13. had promised,
changed 14. did not know, had rented 15. had heard, came

I 1. best 2. better 3. youngest 4. most beautiful 5. worse 6. worst 7. most
difficult 8. more 9. least 10. less 11. smallest 12. happier 13. laziest
14. younger 15. louder

MY FINANCIAL CAREER

B 1. awful 2. self-evident 3. shambled 4. grave 5. irresponsible 6. threshold
7. fetched 8. crumpled 9. presume 10. convulsive 11. ghastly 12. intend
13. wretched 14. astonished 15. thrust 16. reckless 17. fearful 18. gather
19. safe

C 1. led the way 2. swam before my eyes 3. too far gone 4. led the way 5. swam
before my eyes 6. too far gone

D 1. a. interruption b. interrupting c. interrupt d. interrupted
2. a. doubt b. doubting c. doubt d. doubted
3. a. implied b. imply c. implication d. implied
4. a. Swimming b. swimmer c. swam d. swim
5. a. intend b. intentions c. intended d. intending

E 1. a. staring b. presuming c. rising d. snapping e. sitting f. fitting
g. writing h. swimming
2. a. cookies b. wives c. miseries d. families e. ladies f. knives g. stories
h. theories i. valleys j. industries

F 1. I have come to open an account and intend to keep all my money in this bank.
2. The manager got up, opened the door, and called to the accountant.
3. I was too far gone to reason now, and had a feeling it was impossible to explain
the thing.
4. The bank lost the check because the clerk had made a mistake.
5. My check bounced because I had insufficient funds.
6. You may ask the teller for a check or cash.
7. You can deposit money and buy savings bonds in a bank.
8. All banks lend money, but some charge more interest than others.

9. Banks are safe because each account is insured by the federal government.

10. You can withdraw money from your account, but, you cannot withdraw more money than you have in it.

G 1. it's 2. It's 3. its 4. its 5. it's 6. it's 7. It's its, its 8. its 9. its 10. It's, its

I 1. speak 2. want 3. were 4. has 5. has been 6. feel 7. has 8. sleep 9. have 10. wish

OLD COUNTRY ADVICE TO THE AMERICAN TRAVELER

B 1. a 2. d 3. b 4. c 5. a 6. d 7. a 8. d 9. c 10. a 11. d 12. b 13. c

C 1. good 2. well 3. well 4. beautifully 5. serious 6. seriously 7. quietly 8. quiet, quietly 9. badly 10. well 11. short 12. shortly 13. badly 14. penetratingly 15. penetrating 16. slowly 17. slow 18. slowly 19. frantic 20. frantically

D 1. a. Let's study for the test.
   b. Let's meet for lunch tomorrow.
   c. Let's eat in the cafeteria.
   d. Let's give him the information he wants.
   e. Let us not give him the information he wants.

E 1. The tall man who is wearing a blue shirt builds bridges.
   2. Jerry, who was standing at the corner, saw the girl.
   3. Some examples of words that were borrowed from French are *café, garage,* and *menu.*
   4. Prefixes that give them different meanings can be added to some words.
   5. Some mushrooms that look very safe are poisonous.
   6. The lovers, who were holding hands, were running down the street.
   7. Jack and Jill, who were carrying a pail of water, went up the hill.
   8. Give generously to the Red Cross, which is a good cause.
   9. The woman who was standing in the doorway attracted our attention
   10. The picture, which is on the wall, belongs to the art teacher.

F   "Let's say no more about it," the old man said.
   "Yes, sir," my uncle said.
   "Let's not speak of the matter again," the old man said. "It's finished. I have seven children. My life has been a full and righteous one. Let's not give it another thought. I have land, vines, trees, cattle, and money. One cannot have everything—except for a day or two at a time."
   "Yes, sir," my uncle said.
   "On your way back to your seat from the diner," the old man said, "you will pass through the smoker. There you will find a game of cards in progress. The players will be three middle-aged men with expensive-looking rings on their fingers. They will nod at you pleasantly and one of them will invite you to join the game. Tell them, 'No speak English.' "

"Yes, sir," my uncle said.

"That is all," the old man said.

"Thank you very much," my uncle said.

"One thing more," the old man said. "When you go to bed at night, take your money out of your pocket and put it in your shoe. Put your shoe under your pillow, keep your head on the pillow all night, *and don't sleep.*"

THIS YEAR IT'S GOING TO BE DIFFERENT

B   I. 1. j   2. b   3. d   4. c   5. e   6. h   7. g   8. i   9. f   10. a

II. 1. boundless   2. sarcastic   3. spontaneous   4. trivial   5. dreads   6. smart
7. drawn by   8. considerate   9. jovially   10. makes every effort

D   1. a. dreading   b. dreadful   c. dread
2. a. spontaneity   b. spontaneous   c. spontaneously
3. a. performed   b. perform   c. performance   d. performing
4. a. playing   b. player   c. play
5. a. considering   b. considerate   c. consider   d. consideration

E   1. has been studying   2. bought   3. had been working (worked)   4. has been rapping   5. dropped, broke   6. had broken   7. have never kept   8. began   9. has lived   10. has visited   11. lost, have not found   12. became   13. have, contributed   14. lived   15. has given   16. was   17. have studied   18. have never studied   19. had, started, came   20. was wearing, had received

F   1. Before I wrote my list, I read books on self-improvement.
2. Maggie, my wife, was at the sink when I came downstairs.
3. I'd started reading the paper when Sammy, our five-year-old son, came in.
4. He was wearing a watch that he had received for Christmas.
5. In order to establish some kind of rapport, I struck up a conversation with Kit.

A BIRD IN HAND—WHAT'S IT WORTH?

B   I. 1. yes   2. yes   3. yes   4. no   5. yes   6. no   7. no   8. yes   9. no   10. yes

C   1. Who   2. whom   3. Who   4. Who   5. whom   6. whom   7. Who   8. Who, whom   9. whom   10. Who   11. whom   12. whom   13. whom   14. Whom   15. Whom

E   2. Chinese, Chinese   3. Frenchman or Frenchwoman, French   4. Iraqi, Iraqi or Arabic   5. Swede, Swedish   6. Norwegian, Norwegian   7. Greek, Greek
8. Dutchman or Dutchwoman, Dutch   9. Nepalese, Nepalese   10. German, German
11. Dane, Danish   12. Englishman or Englishwoman, English   13. Russian, Russian   14. Japanese, Japanese   15. Italian, Italian   16. Scot, Scotch
17. Irishman or Irishwoman, Irish   18. Pole, Polish   19. Hungarian, Hungarian
20. Turk, Turkish   21. Israeli, Hebrew

YOU WERE PERFECTLY FINE

B 1. monastery 2. tight 3. treat 4. collapse 5. stretch 6. nasty
7. overwhelming 8. stuffy 9. sore 10. corking 11. temple 12. mastiff
13. sock 14. dandy

C 1. false 2. false 3. false 4. true

D 1. a. easing b. easily c. ease d. easy e. eased
2. a. comfort b. comforting c. comfort d. comforted
3. a. insistence, insisting b. insist c. insisted d. insistence
4. a. collapse b. collapsed c. collapsing

E 1. Because I was very hungry, I ate four sandwiches.
I ate four sandwiches because I was very hungry.
I ate four sandwiches; I was very hungry.
2. Dinosaurs, as displayed in natural history museums, were very large creatures.
3. Reading detective stories was Alan's favorite activity, but he felt guilty about not studying.
4. In 1776, the Declaration of Independence was signed.
5. Professor Adams, our new English teacher, is a vibrant and fascinating person.
6. Professor Adams is our new English teacher. He is a vibrant and fascinating person.
7. John had juice, toast, eggs, and coffee for breakfast.
8. In the morning I thought I had lost my wallet; however, I found it in my drawer later in the day.
9. The book he had written became very popular, even though no one understood it.
10. "Look at me." he said, "I bought a new suit."

HARPIST ON HORSEBACK

C 1. making sense 2. bears a strong resemblance 3. stay in touch 4. found my way 5. have my reservations about 6. get hold of 7. to make up with

D 1. a. frustrate b. frustration c. frustrating
2. a. queer b. queerness c. queer
3. a. disparagingly b. disparaging c. disparage d. disparagement
4. a. apprehension b. apprehensively c. apprehensive

E 1. would 2. will 3. will 4. would 5. would 6. will 7. would 8. will
9. will 10. would

F 1. have earned 2. have stopped 3. have gotten 4. have taken 5. have convinced 6. have started 7. have taken 8. have learned 9. have performed
10. have sailed

THE AWFUL FATE OF MELPOMENUS JONES

B 1. c 2. c 3. c 4. b 5. a 6. b 7. d 8. a 9. c 10. d 11. a 12. b 13. a
14. c 15. a 16. d

E I. 1. was bracing 2. was reading 3. was looking 4. were landing 5. was
setting 6. was chatting 7. were playing 8. were waiting 9. was walking
10. was getting

III. 1. She was drinking tea when I called her last night.
2. He was staying home when I invited him to dinner.
3. He was playing with the children when I sent them to bed.
4. They were looking at photographs when I came into the room.
5. I was paying my rent regularly when they tried to evict me.
6. He was spending his vacation at home when he broke his leg.
7. They were walking to the beach when they saw the accident.
8. We were writing a letter to the president of the United States when we heard
the good news.
9. She was leaving the house when the telephone rang.
10. They were going shopping when the unexpected guests arrived.

THE SOFT SELL

E to find 2. buying 3. trying on 4. to knock 5. to encourage 6. to purchase
7. giving up 8. selling, to lose 9. closing 10. to notify 11. knowing
12. understanding 13. paying 14. to be 15. to discourage 16. to get 17. to
risk, insulting 18. to help 19. to sell 20. taking

F 1. advise 2. advice 3. advice 4. advise 5. advice 6. advice 7. advised
8. advice 9. advise 10. advice

GLOVE PURCHASE IN GIBRALTAR

B 1. b 2. c 3. d 4. a 5. b 6. a 7. c 8. a 9. c 10. c 11. a 12. a 13. a
14. b 15. a 16. b 17. d 18. a 19. a 20. b

D 1. a. intrusion b. intruding c. intruded d. intruder e. intrude
2. a. flattery b. flattering c. flattered d. flatterer e. flatter
3. a. absorb b. absorption c. absorbing d. absorbed
4. a. contemplating b. contemplate c. contemplated d. contemplation

WHAT DO YOU DO WITH YOUR OLD COFFEE GROUNDS?

B   1. s   2. g   3. e   4. i   5. o   6. n   7. g   8. j   9. t   10. h   11. f   12. b   13. u
14. a   15. c   16. l   17. r   18. m   19. k   20. p

C   1. took   2. struck   3. sung   4. brought   5. hidden   6. drank, sang   7. knew
8. taught   9. flung   10. shook   11. lay   12. laid   13. lain   14. bought   15. sank
16. lie   17. lay   18. lay   19. lay   20. lay, lie

D   1. a. confronted   b. confrontation   c. confronting   d. confront
     2. a. sympathized   b. sympathetically   c. sympathetic   d. sympathize
        e. sympathy
     3. a. ignored   b. ignorance   c. ignore   d. ignorant   e. ignoring

E   1. a. setting up the screen, adjusting the projector, and sitting down to watch the
        movie
       b. was patient, diligent, and intelligent
       c. class size, cleaning up the halls, and buying new teaching materials
       d. shave and dress

THE ROMANCE OF A BUSY BROKER

C   1. boring   2. romantic   3. curly   4. handicapped   5. sympathetic   6. pompous
7. charming   8. smiling   9. wondering   10. fascinated   11. mysterious
12. loving   13. vibrating   14. angry   15. dangerous   16. poisonous   17. joyous
18. gracious   19. tragic   20. guilty

D   On Monday, John bought one hundred shares of common stock. <u>Afterwards</u>, the
price of the stock started to go up. <u>Consequently</u>, John wanted to sell the stock when
it was two dollars higher than his original cost, <u>but</u> he became greedy <u>and</u> he decided
to hold on to the stock for <u>another</u> few days. He <u>therefore</u> gave orders to his
stockbroker to hold the stock for <u>another</u> month. <u>Then</u> John left for his vacation. <u>As
soon as</u> he left, the price of the stock began to fall. The broker tried to reach John, <u>but</u>
couldn't. <u>Consequently</u>, John lost all his money. <u>As a result</u> of his experience, John
learned not to be greedy.

E   1. a. If he left, we would know it.
       b. If you came late, I wouldn't wait for you.
       c. I would call you if I saw Mother.
       d. If it snowed, we would go skiing.
       e. If the radio broke, Susan wouldn't hear her favorite program.
       f. If the stenographer retired, you would get the job.
       g. I would walk to the park if the weather was (were) nice.
       h. If she loved me, I would propose to her.
       i. If the clock ran quietly, I would buy it.
       j. If there was (were) an earthquake, the town would be destroyed.

UNIVERSITY DAYS (PART I)

B I. 1. k 2. i 3. f 4. g 5. h 6. a 7. e 8. j 9. d 10. b 11. c
    II. 1. c 2. a 3. b 4. d 5. e 6. h 7. f 8. g

UNIVERSITY DAYS (PART II)

B II. 1. j 2. a 3. b 4. i 5. h 6. g 7. e 8. f 9. d 10. c
C 1. take it 2. failed at, took up 3. dish it out 4. get away with it 5. popped up
    6. Shoot over 7. low down 8. on account of 9. Once in a while 10. cut out
    11. fall back on 12. on the ground that 13. a whole lot 14. hunt for 15. dig up
D 1. a. explaining b. explanation c. explain d. explained
    2. a. adjusting b. adjusted c. adjusted d. adjustment e. adjust
    3. a. demand b. demanding c. demanded d. demanding
    4. a. arrange b. arrangements c. arranged d. arranging
E 1. lawyer 2. doctor or physician 3. journalist 4. accountant 5. biologist
    6. chemist 7. economist 8. psychologist 9. artist 10. musician 11. geologist
    12. engineer 13. physicist 14. dramatist 15. pharmacist 16. architect
    17. philosopher 18. historian 19. mathematician 20. linguist
F 1. had not gone, would not have met
    2. had had, would have bought
    3. had known, would have written
    4. had dug, would have gotten
    5. would have enjoyed, had not had
    6. had not failed, would not have taken
    7. had not forgotten, would have praised
    8. had buttoned, would have felt
    9. had arranged, would have finished
    10. had not improved, would not have gone
    11. had not maintained, would have had
    12. would have seen, had stood
    13. had been, would not have needed
    14. would have called, had known
    15. had been, would have passed

COPYRIGHTS AND ACKNOWLEDGMENTS

For permission to use the selections reprinted in this book, the authors are grateful to the following publishers and copyright holders:

THE BODLEY HEAD, London For "My Financial Career" and for "The Awful Fate of Melpomenus Jones" by Stephen Leacock, both from *Literary Lapses (The Bodley Head Leacock)*. Reprinted by permission of the publisher.

ART BUCHWALD For "The Time Killer" from *More Caviar* (1957) and for "The Soft Sell" from *I Never Danced at the White House* (1971), both by Art Buchwald. Reprinted by courtesy of the author.

DODD, MEAD & COMPANY, INC. For "My Financial Career" from *Laugh with Leacock* by Stephen Leacock. Copyright 1930 by Dodd, Mead & Company, Inc., copyright renewed 1958 by George Leacock. Also for "The Awful Fate of Melpomenus Jones" from *Stephen Leacock's Laugh Parade*. Copyright 1940 by Dodd, Mead & Company, Inc., copyright renewed 1968 by Stephen L. Leacock. Both reprinted by permission of Dodd, Mead & Company, Inc.

GERALD DUCKWORTH & CO. LTD., London For "You Were Perfectly Fine" by Dorothy Parker from *The Collected Dorothy Parker* (Duckworth, 1973). Reprinted by permission of the publisher.

HAMISH HAMILTON LTD., London For "University Days," text and illustrations by James Thurber, from *Vintage Thurber*. The Collection Copyright © 1963 Hamish Hamilton Ltd., London. Reprinted by permission of the publisher.

HARCOURT BRACE JOVANOVICH, INC. For "Old Country Advice to the American Traveler" by William Saroyan. Copyright 1939, 1967 by William Saroyan. Text and illustration reprinted from his volume *My Name Is Aram* by permission of Harcourt Brace Jovanovich, Inc.

MARTIN LEVIN For "A Bird in Hand—What's It Worth?" by Elaine Hart Messmer and for "What Do You Do with Your Old Coffee Grounds?" by Howard Lindsay, both from *The Bedside Phoenix Nest*, edited by Martin Levin. Copyright © 1965 by Martin Levin. Reprinted by permission.

J. B. LIPPINCOTT COMPANY For "Harpist on Horseback" from *Quiet, Yelled Mrs. Rabbit* by Hilda Cole Espy. Copyright © 1958 by J. B. Lippincott Company. Reprinted by permission of J. B. Lippincott Company.

LAURENCE POLLINGER LIMITED, London For "Old Country Advice to the American Traveler" from *My Name Is Aram* by William Saroyan. Reprinted by permission of the publisher.

WILL STANTON For "This Year It's Going to be Different" from *The Reader's Digest Bedside Reader —An Anthology of 101 Great Stories* (1970). Reprinted by permission of the author.

HELEN THURBER For "University Days," text and illustrations by James Thurber, from *My Life and Hard Times*. Published by Harper & Row, New York. Copr. © 1933, 1961 James Thurber. Originally printed in *The New Yorker*.

THE VIKING PRESS, INC. For "You Were Perfectly Fine" by Dorothy Parker from *The Portable Dorothy Parker*. Copyright 1929, © 1957 by Dorothy Parker. Reprinted by permission of The Viking Press. Originally appeared in *The New Yorker*.

WOOD/FREEMAN For "The Late Mr. Adams" from *Fourteen for Tonight* by Steve Allen (1955). Reprinted by permission.